THE AMATEUR

The author at work
in the 1940s (*above*)
and in retirement at
home on the Thames
at Chelsea (*below*)

THE
AMATEUR BOATWOMEN

CANAL BOATING 1941-1945

by

Eily   Gayford

B

M & M   BALDWIN
Cleobury Mortimer, Shropshire
1 9 9 6

Bibliographic Note

This book was first published by David & Charles in 1973. This new edition contains the entire text and illustrations from the first edition, with the exception of a drawing from the title page. The opportunity to correct two minor typographical errors has been taken.

To enhance this new edition, we have added a Foreword by Emma Smith, an extract from Bob Menzies' address at the author's Service of Remembrance, a passage from the author's typescript which was excluded from the first edition, 19 pages of extra illustrations from the author's collection, and an index.

Author's Acknowledgements from the 1973 edition

My grateful thanks to Sylvia and John Pyper and Ann Trego Bennett for their help and encouragement; to Naomi Dawson and Carolynne Twyman for help with typing; to Mr and Mrs Ernest Carter for checking details and to Mr Ronald Andrews for giving particulars of the gauging rod.

I would like to thank Time-Life International, *The Times*, I.P.C. Newspapers, G.H.V. Baker, Daphne French, R. Longden, Audrey Pritchard and Angela Rolt for permission to publish pictures.

The two full-page drawings of narrow boats were done by A.J. Lewery.

Publishers' Acknowledgements

We are grateful to David & Charles for permission to reprint the first edition; to Emma Smith and Bob Menzies for their enlightening contributions which give us more insight into the author's life; to John Pyper for his considerable assistance with the new material collected together for this new edition; and the Trustees of Eily Gayford's estate for their encouragement.

Cover designed by David Miller

Foreword © Emma Smith, 1996
Memorial Address © Bob Menzies, 1996
Text © The Executors of Eily Gayford, 1996

ISBN 0 947712 31 3

British Library Cataloguing in Publication Data
A catalogue record is available from the British Library.

Published by M & M Baldwin
24 High Street, Cleobury Mortimer, Kidderminster DY14 8BY

Printed by MFP Design & Print
Longford Trading Estate, Thomas Street, Stretford, Manchester M32 0JT

CONTENTS

ILLUSTRATIONS

Foreword
by Emma Smith

Many people during the Second World War found themselves catapulted into unlikely occupations, but none perhaps was more unlikely than the work undertaken by those young women who, instead of joining up with the Wrens or ATS or some other branch of the uniformed forces, elected to train as cargo-carrying boaters travelling to and fro on the inland waterways of England. The life of a boater being arduous in the extreme and also, for any but the most sure-footed and athletic, not devoid of peril, even fewer of those who volunteered with such initial enthusiasm lasted long. They turned up in high hopes and pretty soon, appalled, and sometimes worse, accompanied by a broken limb, they vanished. Eily Gayford, however—or Kitty, as she was generally known throughout her boating days—endured uniquely the gruelling course from its very inception to its conclusion, and this book is a detailed and vivid account of her undaunted experience.

That it is both accurate in its detail and vivid in its description, I, who was once her pupil, can guarantee. Reading today, at my now advanced age, Kitty's portrayal of a time that had seemed irretrievably remote I become again, miraculously, nineteen. Again, as I read, I feel the throb of the diesel engine, smell its acrid fumes at the bottom of a deep lock, touch the dank sliminess of the lock wall. Strapped round my waist is a broad brass-buckled leather belt with a windlass tucked into it, angle downwards. I can recall exactly the awkward imbalanced weight of the windlass and how rough to the grasp was its newly-forged metal, can hear myself groan aloud as I struggle to heave up a paddle. It's winter, bitterly cold; in boots that scratch and scrape for purchase on the frosty stone of a lockside I'm leaning backwards, pressing with all my strength against one of the huge beams until the enormous gate, as though brought reluctantly alive, begins to move and then, light as a feather, swings open. Or, it's a summer morning south of Birmingham, the surrounding countryside green and beautiful, peaceful, war a distant rumour, and I run barefoot along the tarpaulin-covered top-planks to leap down and on to the tow-path at a bridge-hole. Page by page the nearly forgotten past is conjured up and mile by mile returns to me, fresh as paint; and yes, indeed!—that is just how it was.

In 1943 I joined the Grand Union Canal Carrying Company as a trainee, and Kitty was my teacher. In those days I had no idea how recently she herself had graduated—as she describes here—from my own pitiful condition of total ignorance. I believed she knew all about the hazardous business of handling a pair of narrow boats on the 'cut'; and although she quotes an old ex-boater as saying that for him the learning process never ended, yet my belief was not, I think, wholly mistaken. For during the two years Kitty had spent on the water before I arrived, she had absorbed, in addition to the basic principles of boating, a vast and rich hoard of less quantifiable knowledge: the myths and folk-lore of the boat-people, their idiosyncratic speech, their manners and customs and an invaluable assortment of tips and dodges which members of this tightly-closed society were prepared to pass on by way of practical assistance to an outsider whom they grew to treat eventually as an honoured insider.

Canal boaters were a people within a people. Unremittingly hard-working, they had little communication with the wider world wherein they operated and by which they were barely acknowledged. Few of the boaters had had any formal schooling, most of them none; for the definitive characteristic of their calling was that they should be continuously on the move, and how could schools cope with children who were forever passing by? Those who picked up a smattering of education or the vestiges of literacy did so by sheer determination and will-power in the teeth of nearly insurmountable difficulties. They were a people apart, born on the cut and growing up on the cut, exclusively courting and marrying each other and, when their working days were over, retiring to one of the colonies of their own kind established alongside the cut. The instinctive suspicion accorded them by their fellow citizens, those who read newspapers and dwelt from birth onwards in proper houses of bricks and mortar, was reciprocated. In the docks or coalfields or wharves where the boaters took on board or discharged their cargoes they steadily maintained their separate identity. They were silent, discreet, sharp-witted, observant and proud. This habitual reserve was their only defence against a world in the main hostile, exploitative and largely incomprehensible. For them to have relaxed their guard to the extent of inviting a stranger into their cabins and into the heart of their watchful families said a great deal about Kitty and also about the boaters themselves. It was not simply that they appreciated her grit and her stamina, or even that they liked her. More, much more, they trusted her. Their trust was a compliment that Kitty accepted gratefully and never betrayed.

Her relationship with the boaters, as she makes plain in *The Amateur Boatwomen*, was one of mutual respect. Why Kitty should have respected them she clearly shows in every line. Why they on the other hand respected and felt such affection for her is apparent as well but as it were by accident, unintentionally, for Kitty was no egotist and entirely lacked the vanity of someone who feels the need to present an image of herself in a flattering light. Nevertheless the unpretentious personality of the narrator permeates this blithely straightforward narrative and provides a reason why the canal-boaters, intuitively perspicacious as they were in spotting pomposity or patronage, summed her up correctly and as a consequence gave Kitty their rare ungrudging approval.

Memorably, and I'm inclined to say above all, Kitty was tremendous good fun. Her highly developed sense of the ridiculous had an astringent edge to it, but the wit was never cruel. She could laugh without mocking, and her capacity for enjoyment, liberally shared, her intense interest in people, in what they did and felt and said, was unlimited. Whether as teacher or friend she was always excellent company, and her book reflects its creator.

She writes in a style that has about it an unconsidered quality, as if she were sitting opposite her reader and speaking directly with a view, chiefly, to conveying precise and useful information. But because her eye is so keen and her humour irrepressible the listing of locks and methods of entering and leaving them, the naming of tunnels, the thorough description of narrow boats, their size, length, equipment, cabin furnishings, cargoes —all these matter-of-fact *minutiae* to do with journeying to and fro on the water are illuminated again and again by sudden dabs of brilliant colour, touches of startling observation and imagery. I remember as though I had seen it for myself her glimpse of a certain Mrs Jack Wilson busily hemming curtains while simultaneously steering the butty-boat, sewing machine perched on cabin top; and I recollect how the drama of a disastrous ramming-and-sinking episode is indelibly registered by Kitty's wryly apt comparison between her rescued handbag and an overflowing bucket. Nor shall I cease to cherish her wonderfully poetic picture of horse-drawn boats, unsurpassed, surely, in its power of evocation, that for me captures in a single paragraph the whole—to us wartime girl recruits —mysteriously different atmosphere of life on the cut:

> When they are empty they go like the wind, and there is only the sound of the horses' hooves and the swish through the water. Sometimes when we had tied up and were still in bed, very early in the morning you would hear a horse on the path, perhaps the ring of the shoes on cobble-stones, and the swish of water from the bows of the boat, a shout from the man to steady the horse, and then the whip of the line as he threw it so that it cleared the motor exhaust, the soft flap as it fell on the cabin top, then another whip over the cabin chimney, another shout, the bang of the lock gate and the rattle of a paddle dropping. You looked out, it was quite dark, the stars were shining and you just saw the grey outline of a horse standing patiently and a man drawing the paddle. We didn't get back to bed then, but on with the kettle and after a cup of tea we were off again.

The effect of the Second World War was to alter radically everything that an acquiescent public had previously regarded as immutable. Nothing was afterwards the same as before. The canal system, already counted anachronistic as a means of transporting freight inland and having already been edged by neglect into a state of terminal decline, had its end hastened by larger and more impatient forces of destruction. In that colossal combat the part played by a handful of volunteer women ferrying their loads of steel and coal up and down the cut was tiny; but happening, as it did, to coincide with a moment of cataclysmic change it may serve as a modest marker at a notable turning-point in the socio-economic history of this country. Kitty's book, *The Amateur Boatwomen*, is like a small brightly fluttering flag at the conjunction of our industrial past and future. "Goo stiddy," a wise old boatman said to her once, "but keep gooing." She has left us her unsentimental invigorating testimony of what it was like to work boats on the canals of Britain during those four remarkable never-to-be-repeated years and as long as it continues to be published and read Eily Gayford will 'keep gooing'.

Eily Gayford, 1903 - 1991

from the address given by Bob Menzies
at her Service of Remembrance,
Chelsea Old Church, 5 December 1991

Ernest Robert and Emily Elizabeth Gayford lived at Hadleigh in Suffolk. In 1903 they had a second daughter whom they named Eily, although within the family she was called 'Bird' because of the way she darted about and because she was so lively as a little girl. Later, when she worked on the boats, she became known as 'Kit', and later on, as 'Miss C'. No doubt the River Police (who are with us today) had yet another name for her. Whatever name she may have been given, she remained the same staunch friend.

When she was 14 she was sent to a dancing academy where her elder sister was a teacher. I first met her in 1927 when she came to teach dancing at my private school near Norwich. It was a privileged school but that did not make us as well-mannered as we should have been. Also, as you might imagine, we were not keen on dancing lessons, especially since they were obligatory. Nevertheless, she soon pulled us together because her enthusiasm and vitality were irresistible. Before the first year was up, no end of term supper was complete without her directing the carrying out of a wonderful dance which she called the 'Polonaise'.

During the summer holidays of the 1930s she used to stay with my brother and sister and me at our house in Norfolk. There she organised marvellous treasure hunts, taught us swimming in the river and took us on long cycle rides. My mother and father would say "Take care you don't fall off" but she would encourage us to do more and more exciting things on our bicycles. At that time her brother Oswald was a Squadron Leader in the Royal Air Force, and made an extraordinary pioneer flight to South Africa. This I remember well, because she showed me newspaper articles about it. I do believe that his example and her admiration taught me that life should be an adventure. For Eily, everything was an adventure and she put her whole heart and soul into it.

When the Great Depression fell upon us, she joined the Dental Board as a lecturer, going around the schools. Nobody could suppose that lecturing on dental hygiene would be an exciting thing to do. But she showed great adaptability, and she always brought such zest into all she did that she received many letters congratulating her upon her talks and demonstrations.

Then came the war. In 1941, she joined a friend on a canal boat because at the time canals were making an important contribution to wartime transport. After a while, she moved on to work with a boating family, a part of a very closed community. It was closed because the boaters' livelihood was under threat from other modes of transport, and they were gradually fading away as a profession. But she had such sensitivity, such a capacity to mix and such a marvellous ability to listen and learn that she became a friend to all, and indeed a legend. The she began to train other women to handle boats, so successfully that in 1945 she was awarded the MBE.

Perhaps what was even more remarkable was all that she had learned about the people and their way of life. That is to be found very much in the pages of her book *The Amateur Boatwomen* in which she describes her adventures during those years. Note that the title of the book was not *The Amateur Boatwoman*. She did not just write of herself. Typically, she wrote of 'women'—plural—and 'amateur'. She never considered herself to be a professional, but she dedicated her book to the professionals and she remains a legend amongst those who are still on the canals. She had a great capacity to mix; she did not mind what anybody did or who they were, everybody was equal in her sight.

I went abroad in the 1950s, but when I returned ten years later, I began to visit her on her houseboat 'The Buccaneer'. What more suitable name could she have chosen? It was so much like herself. She lived contentedly on 'Buccaneer', watching the river go by, loving the river, watching the tides turn and the sun rise and set. She demanded no more than the simplicity and beauty of this home which she had made for herself. This was the time when she came to know the River Police. They would call in on her and, I suppose, from the start they realised how attached she was to the river and all that happened on it. At Christmas time she used to make mince pies for them, and they became close friends. They used to take her out and she would take the wheel of their launch. They also showed her the Thames Barrier before it was opened.

It was a simple way of life, and reading her book I was struck by a story which is typical of her. She is talking about the son of a boater who had neither learnt to read nor write and she is surprised that he could not communicate either way. "Oh well," he said "what you've never had, you never misses, do you?" and she thought that to be a splendid philosophy. Indeed, it was very much her own philosophy of life.

Funds were short from time to time so, having no false pride, she got on her bicycle, and began 'charring', which she did under the name of 'Miss C'. I sometimes wondered why she called herself 'Miss C'. perhaps it was that 'C' was short for Carnforth because she had lectured at a school at Carnforth at some stage. The real reason, I think, for calling herself 'Miss C' was not that she was ashamed of the sort of work she was doing, but rather to avoid embarrassing her clients if they found out her real identity. However much she earned, and whatever the state of her finances, she always gave one tenth of everything to charities.

In the 1970s I came to London quite often and we lunched together on her boat. I would come in, and there on the table would be pheasant pâté and a chilled bottle of white wine. "Come along, dear, just a little gin," she would say, and after one or two her nose would begin to glow. Then I would sit down, but she would not. No, she could not listen and participate in what she was being told if she sat down to eat at the same time. I think her greatest gift was this ability to listen to other people, to be interested and to make one feel that nobody else mattered to her. It was not idle listening; she never forgot what she was told. You could give her the name of a person, a child or a relation and next time she would ask after that person and remember what had been said, and any problem he or she was facing. She was always sympathetic. She was also extraordinarily self-sufficient. Not that she did not enjoy the company of neighbours—she got on very well with them, but she did not need them as most of us do. She did adopt, or was adopted by, a cat of no less independent a nature, which she called Catkin.

Once, at a time when I was having marital difficulties, we talked about marriage. She said how difficult it all was, then added "Ah well, I did have my moments, you know, dear, but I simply could not find anything that a man could do for a woman that a woman could not do for herself."

'Buccaneer' began to be a burden in the 1980s. It needed more and more of her time and its maintenance was really becoming too much for her. I was afraid that this would be a calamity. She would have to leave, to leave her beautiful boat and the river she loved. I imagined her misery. But not at all, having made up her mind she set about negotiating the sale, and having bought the boat for a few hundred pounds, she sold it for an immensely higher figure, and was as proud as Punch at having managed to sell it so well. She used that capital to make herself perfectly comfortable again at Rydons, and took proper pride in the fact that she had seen that it was time to go there. Having taken her decision, she had no remorse about it.

It was at Rydons that I visited her during her last two years. She received me in her room with the pâté and wine on the table, preceded by a quick gin. She was so happy, so comfortable. She had her favourite bits of furniture, and her books to read. Perhaps she had never been so comfortable in all her long life, and the staff were very kind. I remember her pointing to a handle on the wall, saying "There, if anything happens, all I have to do is to pull that, and they will come and carry me out to the hospital on the other side of the lawn." Of course, that is what did happen eventually.

The last time I saw Eily was in June, during the Wimbledon Tournament. We went through lunch at an unusual speed, and then she said "Come, come, we must watch Wimbledon on the TV." There she sat before it, eager, excited, and following every stroke, and turning to me she said "You know, I was quite a useful country house player in my time." I am sure that is true. When she saw that I needed my spectacles to watch, she was amazed. "What, you wear spectacles!" she exclaimed. "Why, yes, I'm over 70, you know." "My dear," she said, "quite unnecessary, all you need is eye exercises, as I do, and I don't need spectacles."

The end came in October. She had made all the necessary arrangements, which was typical of her. She left nothing for anyone to worry about. This memorial service was one of her requests, to bring us all together. All her friends, by whatever name we knew her, have gathered to remember her. She also asked that we should sing a favourite hymn—'He Who Would Valiant Be'—and if anybody was valiant it was Eily Gayford.

That same morning, Eily's ashes were scattered on the Thames with some wreaths. I met Mr Jim McCann at the reception after the Memorial Service. He represented the Thames lightermen who felt that she had been so genuine a lover of the river that they had held a special ceremony for her and had offered the lighterman's prayer. Later he wrote to me as follows:

"I am putting on paper the words of the casting of the tide tables and watch on the water. 'Time and Tide waits for none. Wherever the four winds and seven seas take you, Eily Gayford, may you find a safe haven.'"

How it began
(from the original typescript of this book)

When war broke out in 1939, I was with my mother who lived in Suffolk. The job I was in ceased to exist, and for a year I worked on a friend's fruit farm picking, grading and packing apples. This was just right for the time being; there was so much uncertainty during that first year. The war had not really got going and though I hoped to find some other work for 'the duration', I could not just abandon my mother. She lived entirely on her own and was 70 plus, so for that reason I hesitated to enlist in any of the services. What I really wanted was something which would allow me to get back and see her every month. What a hope! and what could I possibly do? I was not qualified or cut out for any of the recognised war work, and the only useful thing I seemed to be good at was riding a bicycle. In fact it all seemed rather hopeless and depressing. I distinctly remember announcing in bitter tones one day "Too young for the first war and now too old for this."

Then one day in March 1941 I got a letter. It was from someone I had not even heard of, and though I did not know it at the time, it made possible, and started me off on, what turned out to be the most satisfying war work. What was more, being an intrepid cyclist, as opposed to a timid one, was a distinct asset. I was able to get home once a month, and even the problem of my mother living alone was solved, as by then we had some very nice evacuees living in the house.

The letter had come from a girl called Daphne who lived near Worcester. She explained that her brother owned a canal boat, powered by a 10 H.P. Petter engine, which she and another girl had started to run as a cargo-carrying concern on the Worcester & Birmingham Canal. They needed a third hand, so would I care to go down for a week's trial trip to see if I liked the work. She added that she had heard of me in a roundabout way from her mate, Molly. Molly's husband had chanced to meet a friend of our family one day in Town and happened to mention what his wife was doing and that they wanted another to join them. Our friend said he thought he knew someone who might do, and there and then gave my name and address, which eventually reached Daphne, who decided to write at once . . . . .

Chapter 1

I BECOME A BOATWOMAN

BEFORE THE Second World War the canals in this country were almost a closed book to the majority of people. Only comparatively few were sufficiently interested to find out about them, or take a boat out on the network of waterways which formed the private world of the canal boat people, and like the majority I was hardly aware of our canal system when the opportunity occurred for me to become a canal boatwoman.

It was early in 1941 that I received a letter from a complete stranger asking if I would like to join her and another girl, and help them to run her cargo-carrying boat on the Worcester & Birmingham Canal. She explained that the boat was a canal narrow boat, called *Heather Bell*, which they had had built by Nurser of Braunston before the war and had used for pleasure boating. The idea now was to operate her for carrying cargo between Worcester and Birmingham, and also on the river Severn.

This was a chance too good to be missed and after innumerable postponements and changes of plan (which I was to learn later are all part of a boater's life) I eventually set out for Worcester on a week's trial. Trial it certainly was in more ways than one: my ignorance, confusion and bewilderment were a sore trial to the other two, as well as being a very great trial to me!

On arrival at Worcester I was told that as Daphne was away on a trip I was to stay the night at her home, as the other girl, Molly, was due back from leave the next day and we could then go up to Cannock and join the boat there, where they were loading coal.

During the evening I was told quite a lot about the boat, but never having seen one, let alone a lock being filled or emptied, there was little hope of my understanding much of what was being said. However one thing was made quite clear, the *Heather Bell* was a canal boat, not a barge, and the people who worked the boats were boaters, not bargees.

The next day I was lent a pillowcase for my belongings as there was no room in the boat for my suitcase, so it and my travelling clothes were left at the house. We then set out for the station to meet Molly and eventually the two of us were on our way to Cannock where we at last arrived rather late in the day.

Then started what seemed to be an endless walk in search of the Cut, which was apparently what everyone called a canal. Molly had been there before, but only by boat, and as it was then getting dark, and no-one seemed to understand where we wanted to get to, it was some time before we at last struck a lane which she remembered. After picking our way over waste ground, railway lines and heaps of slag, we came to a stop, and Molly in a firm tone announced, 'Here are the boats.' As by then it was pitch dark, I had to take her word for it, but she followed it up with 'But the *Heather Bell* isn't there'. Bewildered, tired and hungry, this was not my idea of starting life on the boats. However she then said 'Stay here a minute', and with one step she had disappeared into the blackness. I did 'stay here', literally rooted to the spot, and much too scared to move an inch in case I stepped into the canal, or for all I knew a coal mine.

After what seemed quite half an hour, she suddenly reappeared and said, 'It's quite all right, the *Heather Bell* will be in in the morning, and Mr Arnott says we can go up and sleep on their drawing-room floor'. Well, to me that sounded the height of luxury, and when we stepped into their brightly-lit room with a magnificent fire, and after about two minutes were drinking coffee and eating sandwiches, all the previous depression disappeared in a flash.

Mr Arnott was the manager at the Brownhills colliery, and I shall never forget the kindness shown to us that night by him and his wife. We made up two beds on the floor with rugs and cushions and turned in. I remember thinking how nice it was to go to bed with a fire in the 'bedroom'; the next moment it was morning, and the next thing I learnt was that I snored too much.

Soon after breakfast Mr Arnott told us that *Heather Bell* was in, so out we went, and I had my introduction to her, Daphne and her brother. The cabin seemed to be incredibly small, and I wondered how in the world the four of us were going to sleep in it: however, there was one other cabin—a very minute one in the fore-end which the brother used. From my diary I see that this was April 8th, also that we loaded and tied up at the top of the West Bromwich locks, but quite candidly I can remember nothing of the procedure, only that I was very much in the way, and felt quite useless. Goodness knows what time we tied up, whether we ate anything or even attempted to wash, but we went to bed, Daphne on the cross bed, me on the side bed and Molly on the floor. The floor space was about 2ft wide and 7ft long, part of which was under Daphne's bed across the end of the cabin. The side bed, mine, was a locker or seat on the right hand side.

I must have been still very bemused all the next day, as the entry in my diary is just five words—Tunnel, Tardebigge locks,

tied up. As we would have let go not later than 6 am and not tied
up before 8 pm, during which time there was unceasing activity,
it all goes to prove how utterly bewildering the first days are for
beginners on the boats. The tunnel mentioned was Wast Hill
(King's Norton), which is 2,726 yards long, but as undoubtedly
I was put in the cabin whilst we went through it, my reactions
must have been confined to contemplating the darkness and
thinking 'How marvellous to be going through a tunnel!' Tardebigge is about the longest flight of locks in the country, consisting
of 30, followed almost immediately by another 12, and from
what I remember, it used to take us about two and a half hours
to work through them. 'Tied up' meant a lot. Worn out by then,
and probably thinking that boating consisted only of a turmoil of
going on, on, on and on, but 'tied up' had shown me that at least
we did eventually stop.

The next day we reached Worcester in the morning, the
approach by canal being very dirty and unattractive, and we tied
up at Townsend's flour mill ready to unload the coal. However,
they did not do it that day, so we had time off to get baths and
do some very necessary washing. To wash oneself in the cabin
was by no means easy: the floor space was small, all the hot
water had to be heated in the kettle, which was not very large,
and neither was the bowl which we used.

The day following was Good Friday, and as most of the mill
was on holiday there was some doubt as to whether they would
unload us, but as Daphne was very anxious to load again with
flour the next day, so that we could be under way by Easter
Monday, she decided we would all help. This meant shovelling
the coal out of the boat, over the side into a chute; as the coal
went out we got lower down in the boat, so that we were throwing
each shovelful almost shoulder high.

Then came sweeping and cleaning the bottom of the boat and
replacing all the floor boards. Before the coal had been loaded

these had all been neatly stacked at the fore end and covered with a tarpaulin so that they were clean and dry for the bags of flour which were the next cargo. After that we moved the boat along to the part of the mill where the flour was loaded.

On Saturday morning loading started: the sacks came down a chute. 'Arthur' wheeled them along a short platform, neatly tipped them on to the shoulder of 'Harold' who was standing in the boat and who then stacked them in position. Naturally the men up in the mill sent sacks down the chute very much quicker than Arthur was able to deliver them to Harold, so to prevent an avalanche of sacks piling up on the platform, there was an arrangement of a heavily weighted block of wood at the end of the chute, with a cord attached; when this was pulled the wood was raised and the sack slid straight down and dropped on the platform below; when kept down, it acted as a dam which stopped the sack. All very simple, but complications arose when I was put on to control the cord. All went well for a time, until at the moment of raising the wood to let one sack out, down shot another, which got halfway under the wood before I could drop it back in position. Immediately the next came sliding down pushing the first a little further, followed by another and yet another, and the whole lot steadily slipping. I was quite powerless to stem the flood. Why couldn't Arthur go a bit quicker, and why couldn't the man above be a bit slower? At last the whole proceedings had to be checked while Arthur came to my rescue.

After the loading was finished the next performance was to sheet up the boats. The length of the cargo space was divided into four sections known as the Stern End, Stern Middle, Back of the Mast and the Fore End. These divisions were made by three cross beams. The one between the Fore End and Back of the Mast supported the mast—a large square piece of timber, partly hollow, into which fitted the steel mast which could be raised about 2ft and held in position by a steel pin. The other

B

two beams each had a stand—like a plank of wood—which went through a slot in the beam and rested in a groove in the keelson.

When a boat was towed from the path, the line was attached to the mast as the pull coming that distance away from the bows enabled the boat to be steered. Top planks were placed on the stands to form a cat walk the entire length of the cargo and level with the cabin top. Short side cloths which were kept rolled up along the gunwale were then pulled up and the strings attached to them taken over the top planks, laced through eyelets on the opposite cloths and finally pulled taut and tied over the planks. The whole cargo was then covered in with the top cloths—four large tarpaulin sheets which came down over the side cloths and these again were tied down with innumerable strings. Sheeting up, I soon learnt, was easily and quickly said but in practice it was a slow and tedious business.

We then moved along through two locks, tying up above the second, which was called the Block House, but usually pronounced Block'us. The reason why we did this was because as we were not going to start the trip until the Sunday afternoon, it was a more agreeable place to be tied up. I did not notice very much difference though, as it was extremely dirty and squalid, but we were free from the throb of the mill which worked night and day, also the smell from the stables, plus the rats.

Molly had gone to Town in the morning, and as Daphne had gone home I had the boat to myself for the night. The next morning being Sunday represented the first lull in activity since the previous Monday, so I was able to sit back, take stock of my surroundings and enjoy being on my own. It was very pleasant sitting in the cabin eating my breakfast and looking out through the open doors along the canal.

The *Heather Bell*'s cabin was just the same as all other canal boats. To enter it you stepped down one step on to the floor which was about 2ft wide and 7ft long the headroom roughly

5ft 7in. As there was so little floor space you generally sat down at once, either on the coal box which was actually the step, or on the side bed, the locker on the right hand side. Sitting there and immediately facing you was the stove, a miniature range complete with oven and as it was so close you could easily poke the fire without getting up. If you slid yourself a few inches along the locker you were then in front of the table cupboard, the door of which opened downwards to form a table and below was the knife drawer. Next to this was the bed cupboard, $3\frac{1}{2}$ft wide, and when the door was let down it rested on the edge of the locker opposite and formed the double bed.

The real boaters generally kept the cross bed permanently in position and made up, but we used to stow all the bedding in the cupboard part and keep the door closed so that we had a little more room. Above it were two small cupboards, and at floor level two good sized drawers. Drinking water was kept in a 4-gallon can on the cabin top and a bucket in the engine room served as a lavatory. The whole of the interior was painted brown and grained and profusely decorated with the traditional boating design of red, pink and yellow roses. On the door of the table cupboard was the 'landscape'—a bright painting of a castle, mountains and water. The same landscape and roses were painted on the panels of the two cabin doors. China and a certain amount of food were kept on the shelves in the table cupboard, and under the counter—the small deck on which you stand to steer—there was a good space in which to keep the rest of the household stores.

The engine room came next to the cabin, and to approach it you walked round either side of the cabin on a gunwale $3\frac{1}{2}$in wide. On the cabin top, which is the roof of the cabin and engine room, was the slide, a wooden shutter which pulled over the space just inside the cabin doors. On its front edge was a hasp, so that when pulled over and the doors closed it could be padlocked to a staple on one door, and the cabin securely fastened. On the extreme left of the cabin top was the chimney of the cabin stove, and directly behind it stood the water can, also painted with the rose design. Directly over the engine, a raised ventilator for the engine room, and also another chimney for the engine exhaust. I took in all this with very great interest and began to feel I was in a way part of everything, instead of having that outside feeling of being on the surface and not really belonging.

The *Heather Bell* was identical with all motor-driven narrow boats, except that her measurements were slightly less owing to the fact that they wanted to be able to take her on the Welsh canals, where the locks are rather smaller than usual.

At the end of 1940, Daphne decided to try running her as a regular cargo carrying craft, and, if successful, to continue doing so while the war lasted. At that time Daphne's boating experience was confined to acting as mate to her brother when they took the *Heather Bell* out at weekends and for holidays; they had occasionally carried cargo, but not regularly, and their boat and boating was essentially a hobby and pleasure. Under those conditions, things were taken in quite a light-hearted manner, and as Daphne often used to say, she had never had any of the responsibilities, so was lacking in experience when deciding to run the *Heather Bell* on her own.

The first thing to do was to get a crew, so she advertised, and eventually got in touch with Molly. Molly was extremely capable and efficient, and had had considerable sailing experience, and as soon as she had arranged to work with Daphne she did a course on the maintenance of Petter engines. Together, they organised and fitted out the *Heather Bell*, and with one other to complete the crew, they at last got going. The 'other one' varied, as amongst the answers to her advertisement were people who volunteered to help temporarily for various reasons, and several had come and gone before Molly joined in March.

They had only made a few trips when I arrived in April, so they were still quite inexperienced.

My first impressions on joining the boat were the dirty conditions in which we lived, and the chaotic frenzy in which we progressed. This was inevitable and not surprising. How could they expect to be organised and efficient in the cabin and at the same time be equally efficient at handling the boats when they had so little experience of either? Besides we were overcrowded—three people, sometimes four, in one motor boat.

I came up against exactly the same problem later on when taking over my own pair of boats and three trainees. I still have a humiliating snapshot showing my cabin top looking like a kind of junk yard with ropes and lines all over the place and the bicycle mixed up with the lot, and goodness knows what state the cabin was in.

The handling of a canal boat requires a certain amount of skill and a considerable amount of experience. The overall length is about 70ft, the beam 7ft, and to steer this great length round some of the incredible bends and corners on the canal appears almost impossible and the beginner finds it very often is! You soon learn that the canal is seldom, if ever, a uniform depth from side to side. If it were, steering the boat would be comparatively easy. As it is you have only to get the rudder caught in mud to find that all control is lost and the bows career madly into the bushes and undergrowth on the bank, or, worse still, the whole boat gets completely 'stemmed up'—stuck on the mud. This does not always happen in a rural setting either. The bend you fail to negotiate is sometimes part of a factory, or a concrete wall with the odd iron pipe or girder sticking out of it; then, to avoid the sickening grinding and scraping along the side of the boat, one of us would dash along the top planks with a sausage shaped fender to lower at what appeared to be the best spot to soften the blow.

If we got badly stemmed up we made superhuman efforts to shaft her off, but as the long shaft (boat hook) was twelve feet long it was almost too heavy for me to lift, let alone use to any advantage. An alternative method was to try and haul her off with the cotton line, though this would depend on her position and whether we could get on to the bank or towpath. Both these activities were physically hard and exhausting, and then there were meals to be prepared, cooked and eaten under rather difficult conditions and with constant interruptions, so altogether there was wear and tear on nerves as well as bodies and it was always a great relief to me when we tied up for the night.

But this was a first trip, and I was going through all the bewilderment and confusions which everyone experienced in those days when starting life as a canal boat woman. At that time no book had been written which could give help and guidance to the beginner. Pleasure boating was practically unknown and the canals were the private and secluded world of the professional boaters.

My future was anything but bright and clear on the horizon. The present was what counted and the daily acceptance of everything about this new and unfamiliar life.

Chapter 2

FROM WORCESTER TO CANNOCK

TO RETURN to that Easter Sunday morning; after breakfast I had had a good clean up of the cabin, polished the brass rings round the chimney, and filled up the water can at the lock-keeper's cottage. Molly got back from London, and later Daphne came down from the house with a good supply of vegetables, milk and other perks—our rations had been bought on the Saturday—so we were all set for letting go. This time it was the full trip—Birmingham, Tipton, across to Cannock and home. A distance of about eighty miles, which would probably take us about five days. That time included unloading, loading, and any delays that might be incurred. We also had to go through about 140 locks, so the time was not so slow as might at first appear.

We soon cleared the outskirts of Worcester, and out in the country it was very beautiful. I was allowed to try my hand at steering, which is easy once you have got used to having nearly 70ft of boat in front of you, but most of the time Daphne took the tiller herself, and Molly and I acted as mates. We had got to

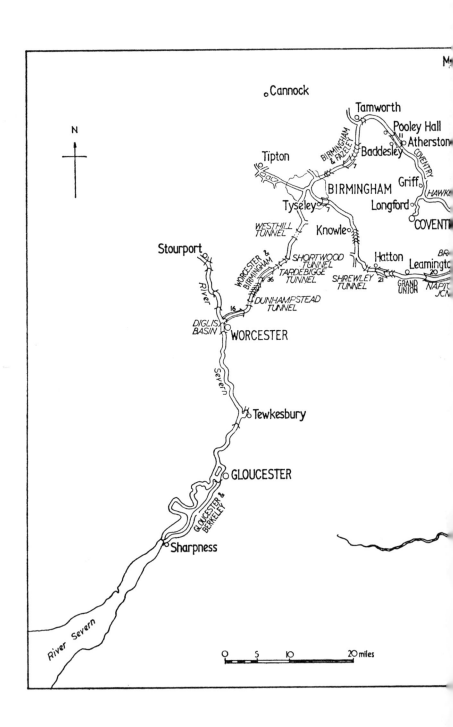

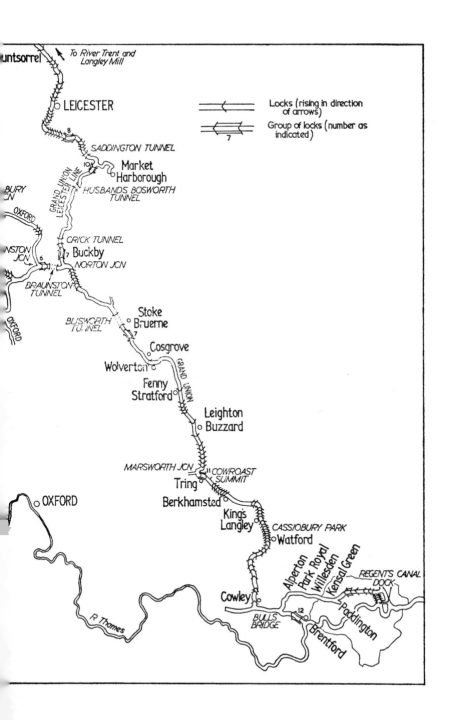

cover thirty miles before reaching Birmingham, including 58 locks and 5 tunnels.

One of the most important duties of a mate is to act as a 'hobbler'. This means going ahead on the towpath to prepare the locks ready for the boat to enter. To do this, you usually step off while going under a bridge, as then the boat is able to get close into the side, and it is easy to jump off even with a bicycle tucked under your arm.

Locks are like the steps of a staircase, and are constructed where there is a rise or fall in the land over which the canal passes. The steeper the rise, the closer together they come, but sometimes they are quite a distance apart. But whatever the distance, the water between any two locks is called a pound. When acting as a hobbler it is just too bad if you are unfamiliar with the route, as you may find yourself getting off too soon, and having to walk an unnecessary distance before the lock is reached.

The working of a lock is a simple affair, but if you are quite ignorant about locks when you start boating, they can be very bewildering. A lock is ready when the water in it is the same level as the pound on which your boat is travelling. To make a lock ready for a boat which is travelling uphill, the hobbler has to shut the top gate, or gates, and drop the paddles. Paddles are like shutters (similar to the flood gates of a mill) which are under the water; they are closed when the paddle is dropped, and the top end of the lock is then completely sealed. The hobbler then goes to the lower gates, and draws or lifts the paddles which release the water from the lock into the pound below. This is done by placing a windlass, rather like the starting handle of a car, only more solid, on the spindle of a bar attached to the lock gate, and turning it. The hobbler then crosses over the gates and does the same thing on the other side. When the water in the lock is level with the pound below the gates can be opened; the lock is then 'made ready' and the boats can pass straight in.

A good road means that every lock you come to is in your favour, or made ready. A bad road is just the opposite—every lock is against you and has to be either emptied or filled before the boats can enter, so your work is doubled. A motorist too can have a good or bad road according to the traffic lights.

I remember what a nightmare hobbling was to me, with no bicycle during those first few trips. I used to race like a madman up to the lock, arrive there gasping for breath, with heart thumping and knees shaking, and then wonder what in the world had to be done with the wretched thing. Having wasted a few precious seconds in coming to a decision, I would then continue the mad race, up to the top gate, shut it, drop the paddle, back to the bottom gate, up with the paddle, cross over the gates and tug and strain at the other in a frenzy of zeal. Then a merciful lull while the water was running out and I sank wearily on to the balance beam, the top part of the lock gate extending as a long beam out over the lock side, which is pulled or pushed to open or close the gate. The rest is not for long, for what do I see but a beastly paddle still up on the top gate, so that not only is water running out of the lock, but into it as well! Off again, and down with the brute, and an agonised look to see if Daphne were round the bend and would have spotted this unforgivable sin of 'wasting water'. Thank goodness she was not, and the next minute I had the gates open and all was as it should be as the boats came into sight. All, except for the poor hobbler, who by then was pounding doggedly along to the next lock.

Later on, while working with the Grand Union, I was to learn that wasting water was a much more serious crime owing to the amount of traffic. A paddle left up, or not completely dropped, could lower the level of the pound above to such an extent that boats would have difficulty in getting through. If this happened, a report would go to the canal engineer, like this: 'I have to report that one of the mates left up a lower gate paddle at Lock

57 and wasted about 6 locks of water. She was on ahead of the boats and was filling locks when at Lock 57 she closed the lower gates and raised all the upper paddles, but omitted to drop one of the lower gate paddles. The locks remained in this state for some time before she realised that the pound above was running empty.' And the engineer would write me a 'this hurts me more than it hurts you' letter, with a suitable reprimand. Leaking lock gates could also cause wastage, but thank goodness that was something for which we were not responsible!

There was one occasion with the *Heather Bell* when I really did waste water with a vengeance, and it is quite impossible even to work up an excuse for it. I arrived at the lock—I must have been in a trance, but anyway I forgot to shut the top gate, and then drew both the bottom paddles. I probably stood there several seconds watching the merry rush and swirl of water, when with a sickening jerk I was brought back to consciousness by suddenly realising what was happening. Water was not just running out of the lock, but the whole pound above was rushing clean through it. This was terrible, and I got the top gate shut in record time. It was no good hoping that Daphne would not notice what I had been up to, as it was only too apparent that the pound above had been lowered.

Another painful episode was when I gaily went off to get a lock ready, and on arrival discovered that I had forgotten to bring a windlass. However, hobbling is not always like that. Once you know what has got to be done, and have generally calmed down, it can be very pleasant indeed.

Even after nearly thirty years, certain details of those Worcester-Birmingham trips are as clear as if I were there only last week. Lock-wheeling up Tardebigge in the summer— lovely sun, unspoilt country, no people milling about, very few houses to be seen, and no other boats; the amount of magpies one saw—far too many to count and worry about; the almost deafening singing of the yellow hammers; so many wild roses we always had a bowl of them on the cabin top; each lock looking just like a narrow slit, and the long, black tarpaulined boat gliding in with only a few inches to spare on either side; the lock where a number of very inquisitive ponies used to come quite close to the boat to watch, and even follow our progress, and the last lock of all, the top lock, deeper than any of the others, the tremendous height of the wet glistening walls and the *Heather Bell* looking so small far away down at the bottom. Then little by little she steadily rose until level with the pound above and we were off again.

Activity seemed to be continuous the whole way up to Birmingham; the locks, of course, kept us on the go, and even in the long pounds there was always something to do—mugs of cocoa and pieces of bread and jam to prepare for elevenses (which was usually 9.30), the cabin to clean, a meal to prepare and cook, wash out a few clothes, the engine to see to and clean, or if the boat had a list, crawl under the top cloths and hump and heave some of the sacks until she was level again. Always something, even if it was only making up the fire, or filling the coal box. Quite often when we saw a nice farm, one of us would dash off to see if they would let us have some milk. This was rather fun and we used to acquire our own special friends, but the worst part was trying to catch up again with the *Heather Bell* while carrying a full milk can. It was then that she seemed to travel very fast, and you wondered if you would ever be able to overtake her before the next bridge. If you did not it might mean walking another half mile or more to the one beyond.

We seldom saw any other boats until we got into Birmingham, which was probably just as well, as the Worcester & Birmingham canal is narrow and shallow. To use a boater's expression, 'the bottom was too near the top'.

I did not get to know much about the tunnels during those

first trips, as Daphne or Molly always steered through them. I was more out of the way if I stayed in the cabin, but I was always rather impressed with the preparations before going through King's Norton, the longest one. First the headlamp had to be fixed on the fore-end and tested, and then the steerers would dress up in oilskins and sou'westers, because there were so many drips and cascades. When in the tunnel I would look up at the shining figure whose tense face was faintly illuminated by the light in the cabin, and think how clever and brave she was. Of course, as always happens, by the time I was taking the boat through tunnels myself, it no longer seemed either brave or clever, which was most disappointing. One of the shorter tunnels through which we passed always fascinated me. When we were about three boat lengths from the end, the arch of the tunnel was so clearly reflected in the water, and the water was so still, that the effect was exactly as if the boat were gliding along through the centre of a circular tube.

The approach into Birmingham was very dirty and squalid for some distance, and slightly worse at the Bar Lock, which is the end of the Worcester canal right in the centre of Birmingham, just off Broad Street. There we were checked through by the Toll Office man, and continued on our journey to Tipton. We were now in the centre of the network of waterways round Birmingham, and I never knew how Daphne could remember the various turnings we took. The rest of the way to Tipton was purely industrial, but there were no locks until quite at the end. These three were singularly unattractive, and it was quite usual to pick up a motor tyre, rope or any odd piece of clothing on the blades of the propeller. It seemed to be the practice of the people living in the houses by the canal side to use the cut as a convenient dumping ground for all their junk. When this happened there was a great performance feeling under the counter with the shaft and trying to hook and drag the obstruction off.

The warehouse where we were to unload was opposite the top lock, and usually after tying up we unsheeted the boat, and they started to unload us at once. On this occasion, however, we were not to unload until the next day, so there was no rush. We had the rest of the day to ourselves and went to the pictures in the evening. This was very pleasant, as I was beginning to find the evenings in the cabin rather trying owing to the heat. Because of the blackout, we had to keep the slide pulled over and the doors shut, and as the fire had to be kept up for cooking it used to become suffocatingly hot.

The next morning unloading started soon after ten. The method was rather simple: a chain was lowered into the boat, and when it had been fixed round the neck of a flour bag, men pulled on it, up went the bag and down came the other end of the chain ready for the next. Daphne generally preferred to do the chain on the sacks herself, so Molly and I went out to do the shopping. On our return there were only a few sacks left in the bottom of the boat, and as the last one started to go up, out shot a rat. Molly hurled something at it and killed it, much to the amazement of the men above. If she hadn't I am quite sure one of them would have had to come down to deal with the situation!

After we had swept up, rolled the side cloths, and generally tidied up, we let go and got as far as Walsall Wood. We were off the next morning at six and completed the rest of the run to Cannock. This being my second appearance, I was able to take in more of my surroundings, and also the method of loading. Everything had a rather dreary look about it, and there was the continuous shuffling and grinding of trucks either coming from or going to the pit-head, which was some distance away.

The canal ended here, so the boat had to be turned round before we could set off again. To enable you to do this, the canal had been widened at one point which allowed just enough room to get her round. This is called 'winding' the boat. Strange to say, the water here was crystal clear, so as soon as we had tied up we had a look to see if there was anything on the blades. On one occasion I gaily said to Daphne, 'Yes, there's something here,' hooked the shaft into it and gave a pull, only to drop it the next second as it was the remains of a cat. Then, war or no war, I flatly refused to do anything more about it. I never looked at the blades again after that with quite the same amount of confidence as previously.

Tied up on both sides of the canal for some distance were a great number of day boats, or Joey boats as they were also called. These were horse-drawn, and though they had a small cabin, the men did not often sleep on them, but went home each night after putting up their horse in one of the canal-side stables.

Before the boat was loaded, we had to pick up all the floor boards and stack them up in the fore end, so that they kept clean and dry. The floor boards, or false bottom, are made in square sections which fit between the side of the boat and the keelson; there were thirteen on each side. I found them very unpleasant to handle. They were very heavy to lift, and the underneath side was always wet and oily. After picking them up we slid them on their sides up to the fore end—but even this had its hazards, as you were forced to crouch in an ape-like position when going under the three beams which go across the boat, and under which are tightly braced chains. Invariably I straightened my back before clearing them, with the result that the knobs down my spine were continually being grazed.

The loading was very quickly done, the coal coming down a chute which was directly above the boat, so all that was necessary was to move her slowly along as it poured in. This time we were taking 21 tons of 'beans'; I also learnt that sometimes we took 'peas' and sometimes 'pearls'. They all looked very much the same, and undoubtedly, without being told, I would have grouped them all as 'slack'. While the loading was going on, everything

Working boats: (*above*) *Heather Bell* unloads flour at Tipton; (*below*) sheeting up in Regent's Canal dock

Working boats: (*above*) loading coal at Longford;
(*centre*) a lock in winter; (*below*) and in summer

got coated in coal dust and it was most necessary to keep the cabin and engine room doors shut. However, coal dust is a good clean dirt, and it was surprising how quickly we got everything cleaned up once we were under way.

By this time I was answering to the name of Kid; rather unsuitable, I thought, considering that I was older than either of the other two, but it was quite usual for boat men or children, when working or playing together, to call each other Kid, so no-one appeared to think it odd, and Kid I remained for about two years, when I noticed that it gradually changed to Kit or Kitty.

We were back again in Worcester in the same time that we had taken before, but though slightly less bemused, I was still very much the 'odd man out'. Cooking was proving rather a stumbling block to me, I knew very little about it, and disliked what I did know. However, Molly was very patiently giving me some good tips and teaching me some easy dishes so I was beginning to do my share, but not very well. I realised then, but even more when looking back on it, what a trial I must have been.

The other two were working desperately hard but they lacked experience, and somebody worse than themselves was next to no help at all. I could not do anything to the engine, which used to need constant attention; I was always letting out the fire; I fell in (admittedly only up to the knees, having caught hold of the cabin top) but one of them had to help pull me out; I put Molly's shoes in the oven to dry and forgot them, and I never seemed to be in the right place at the right time. However, I had not been told to go. There was a lot about boating which I did not enjoy, but I had begun to feel that magnetic fascination which is inseparable from the boats. It is hard to define but it is very real.

At about this time, my mother later reminded me, I wrote home and said 'This is all an amazing experience, and most

c

interesting, but I do not think it will become my life work'. Little did I then guess that it would, at any rate for the next five years, which were five of the best, and ones which I shall never forget.

Chapter 3

LAST TRIP TO SHARPNESS

OUR NEXT trip was to Sharpness, and this I was to discover was much more of a lotus-eating period for the mates, as there were no locks, or rather, none for us to work. The Worcester end of the Worcester & Birmingham canal is at Diglis basin, where there are two large locks, the last leading into the river Severn. These were the first large scale locks I had seen, and they seemed enormous after the narrow ones on the canal. However, there was no question of us having to work them, so while the others were preparing to let go I was sent round to Mr Denny Watton, who lived at the Toll House, to ask him to get them ready for us. This he proceeded to do in a most calm and unhurried manner, and I remember him laughing at me as I was in such a fever lest they were not ready in time and kept Daphne waiting. Of course they were, but even after that I never could persuade myself that it was quite unnecessary to do everything at the double. I had been so schooled in the necessity of having locks ready so that the boat was not kept waiting, that I felt obliged to run everywhere to make up for being slow at drawing paddles.

The first part of the river was not very pretty, as the banks

were too high to be able to see what was beyond them, but looking back at the Malvern Hills and the exceptionally green grass
was beautiful. Further on the banks were very steep, high, and
densely wooded in parts. There were a lot of craft on the Severn,
and we were meeting tankers, grain boats, and canal boats of the
Severn & Canal Carrying Co, which worked in pairs. We were
also overtaken by the big boats coming down empty, having
probably unloaded at Stourport, Daphne told me. All this was
fascinating and such a contrast to the canal. The Tewkesbury
lock seemed enormous, and we were herded in with so many
other boats of all sizes that there was no space between any of us.
At other times we were the only boat, and then there was an
unpleasant business of holding on to chains to keep the boat close
in to the side. These chains hung down from the top of the wall,
and as the boat got lower and lower you were left with your arm
nearly pulled out of its socket, and wondering whether you were
supposed to let go or hold on and find yourself in mid-air
dangling against the slimy lock wall.

The next stretch of river to Gloucester was very much the
same, and at Gloucester there was another lock which took us
up into the Berkeley Ship Canal to Sharpness where there is
another even bigger lock out into the river again.

The river between Gloucester and Sharpness is 28 miles and
difficult and dangerous to navigate owing to shifting sands. The
Berkeley Ship Canal, which was opened in 1827, not only reduced
this distance to 16 miles over a level canal, but also allowed for
the passage of far larger boats.

Like all other docks, those at Gloucester are absorbingly interesting, and I do not think I shall ever forget them as they were
the first I was privileged to enter, by boat and in a working
capacity. Previously I had spent many hours as a 'gongoozler'*

*An old canal word for a spectator.

in different docks all over the country, but the difference is quite incomparable. On this first occasion, though, I was still struggling in my sea of bewilderment and so occupied in trying to appear competent that I missed most of the pleasure and interest of the later trips. Just two things remain clearly in my mind before we entered the dock. One, the word 'Gopsil' in huge lettering high up on an enormous warehouse, and the other, the two neat little patches on the seat of the trousers of one of the lock keepers, where holes had been worn by constantly pushing against the balance beams of the lock gates.

After arriving at Sharpness we got the boat ready and were loaded with 25 tons of wheat in bulk. The sheeting-up which followed was a nightmare, as there was a very high wind. I began to wonder if we ever would be able to get the top cloths on and securely tied down. However, nothing blew away, nobody fell in, and at last we were off again. On that homeward trip, I distinctly remember bowling along the Severn in brilliant sunshine and all eating the most delicious fricassé out of mugs. Molly was a marvellous cook and taught me how to make the necessary white sauce, and 'fric' became one of the favourite dishes on the *Heather Bell*. Like all boaters we were issued with emergency ration cards, but because we sometimes travelled on tidal waters we were entitled to seamen's rations as well as our usual allowance. From what I remember they were at least double of everything. In fact we could not afford to buy all we were entitled to. There were only certain shops where you could get these vast supplies and I think we used to go to a little shop near the docks at Gloucester where there was a sticker on the window saying 'Seamen's Rations'. I think it must have been on that first trip to Sharpness that I innocently took some snapshots. What they were I can't remember, but on the way back we were aware of two police cyclists on the bank following us. When they got within shouting distance we learnt it was the camera they were after!

They took it away saying I could have it back after they had developed the film. It turned out to be a lot of trouble for nothing as when I eventually went to collect it, they told me that the whole film was over-exposed!

Back at the Mill at Worcester, and after the wheat was unloaded, we all took part in the delightful pastime of cleaning the boat. Grains of wheat get into every crack and pour through any small hole, all the floor boards had to come up—the wheat underneath smelt, and was starting to grow. However, at last we got it done, but however well we did it, there were always bright green blades of wheat growing up from odd cracks and crannies during the next trip, and we used to consider that another load of coal was the only thing which would really clean it out.

We made several trips to Sharpness. On one, I remember we tied up at some place on the Severn and immediately, plop plop, on to the cabin top came the rats! However, as Daphne had experienced this before, we were equipped with pieces of wire netting to put over the open cabin hatches. Oddly enough that place and the mill at Tipton were the only times I ever had experience of rats actually on the boat.

On another trip we arrived at Gloucester in time to go to evening service in the Mariners' Chapel, which is in the dock yard. There we heard this prayer which is, I believe, the only one for canal boaters:

O thou who didst make for the Children of Israel a highway through the Promised Land, we pray thee to bless the highways of this country, especially its canals and waterways. We would remember before thee all who trade thereon. Be thou to them a Father, a Saviour and a Guide. Bless all who work amongst them for their spiritual good. Guide them by the light of thy Holy Spirit that many souls may be won for Christ. We ask this for thy own Name's sake.

Amen.

This prayer was written by the Rev W. Asbury Smith in 1940, at the request of some friends of the mission.

On our next trip to Birmingham, we again tied up for the night at the 'Block'us' before we started. Daphne went home for the night, and after Molly and I had had our supper, I collected an armful of belongings to take along to the fore cabin where I was going to sleep. It was a pitch dark night, and I stepped out of the brightly lit cabin on to the towing path, and started to walk along to the fore end, having forgotten that as there was a curve in the canal only the two ends of the boat were close to the path. The next second I had walked into the water, having chosen one of the filthiest parts of the cut. I was only up to my armpits, so managed to hold on to my armful of clothes, and Molly came to the rescue. The mud and water were filthy, and how I stank! Molly, who had just started going to bed, then and there washed out all my things which was more than noble of her, and I very shamefacedly slunk off to bed.

That trip went off very much the same as the others; we took the usual five days, and that meant we were nearly always working more than twelve hours a day. All the lock-keepers were very friendly to us, and I found that as a hobbler one acquired even more friends. Until we were in the Birmingham area we saw very little of other boats, but once there we were constantly meeting pairs, most of them belonging to Fellows, Morton & Clayton. These boats were always referred to as Jossers. An abbreviation of Joshua, the name of one of the founder members of the firm.

Round about West Bromwich there were always a lot of the horse-drawn day boats carrying coal. Two men, or a man and a boy, managed these boats—one steered and the other was the 'driver' and also did the hobbling. One special friend of mine had the *Seagull* and he always called me 'Me old flower'. This used to amuse Daphne very much; sometimes as we were going along there would be a raucous shout from some murky opening at a factory where coal was being shovelled out of a boat. 'Har yer gittin' on, me ol' flower?' Then there was the old Scotsman who lived near one of the locks, and used to come out and talk while we were getting the lock ready. He once recited the following little rhyme:

'Full steam ahead', the Captain cried.
The engineer from the bank replied
'The donkey's doing his best.'

We thought this must have been in reference to the time when they first started having steam-driven canal boats.

There is something very fascinating about horse-drawn boats. When they are empty they go like the wind, and there is only the sound of the horses' hooves and the swish through the water. Sometimes when we had tied up and were still in bed, very early in the morning you would hear a horse on the path, perhaps the ring of the shoes on cobble-stones, and the swish of water from the bows of the boat, a shout from the man to steady the horse, and then the whip of the line as he threw it so that it cleared the motor exhaust, the soft flap as it fell on the cabin top, then another whip over the cabin chimney, another shout, the bang of the lock gate and the rattle of a paddle dropping. You looked out, it was quite dark, the stars were shining and you just saw the grey outline of a horse standing patiently and a man drawing the paddle. We didn't get back to bed then, but on with the kettle and after a cup of tea we were off again.

It is only a cotton line which is used for towing these boats, and it is amazing how the friction from these lines will wear deep grooves in the wood of the lock gates, the stone work at the edge of the locks, and even in iron. On the towing path side of the bridges pieces of iron are placed against the brick sides as a protection and this iron is often worn into such deep grooves that the effect is like jagged teeth. It seems almost impossible that it is caused entirely by the friction of a cotton line.

Back at Worcester and unloaded we moved round into Diglis basin. Here we tied up quite near a large boat which had been converted into a signal training ship for boys joining the Royal Navy. HMS *Bounty* was very kind to us, and we often had cups of tea sent across when we had been working on the *Heather Bell* and were too busy to stop and boil the kettle.

Molly now left for a few days in London, so Daphne decarbonised the engine, and I was put to various cleaning and painting jobs. By the time we were ready to start again, Molly was unable to return so Daphne decided we would try to do the trip by ourselves. At that time this was quite a momentous undertaking as never before had the two of them made a whole trip entirely by themselves. We decided that if we went very carefully we ought to be able to manage. This was in 1941, and in 1945 it seemed quite extraordinary that we should have even hesitated about doing it; however, at the later part of 1942, I remember just the same kind of weighty discussion between another girl and myself as to whether we should make the epoch-making decision of taking the pair of boats only two-handed for a whole day! By 1944 I think every pair of boats manned by girls had, at some time or another, been taken two-handed from London to Birmingham, Coventry and back as a matter of course.

Well, off we went, and back we came, admittedly having suffered a few headaches, but otherwise all went well, and we then decided that a crew of three was too many, and that when Molly was on I was off, and *vice versa*. I then went home for a period of leave, and Molly returned. This time, instead of doing the usual Birmingham run they went down the River Severn to a place between Gloucester and Sharpness, to carry stone. This meant they were working on a tidal part of the river and I very much regret that I was never able to share this new experience.

During that leave I reorganised my boat clothes. Underwear got terribly dirty and owing to the difficulties of washing and drying, it was steadily becoming a clerical grey, so boys' pants and vests seemed to be the most sensible thing to invest in and I dyed one pair bright blue and the other red. My trousers, too, were just about worn out, so I cut down a pair of my brother's bell bottoms, over from the first war, and made the jumper into a jacket. Armholes and sleeves were no good unless they were loose—both sleeves in my leather jacket were practically out—and later on one of the glove manufacturers in Worcester very kindly gave me three leather skins which I forced the dressmaker at home to make into a kind of loose shift which proved indispensable and lasted until the end of the war.

I also got some instruction in the throwing of ropes and lines. This had always been a constant nightmare to me as they never seemed to go in the right direction, or if they did, always fell short. As luck would have it a friend who sailed a lot happened to be home on leave at the same time, so taught me, and made me practise until I could not only throw a line from far or near so that it was possible for him to catch, but also high up over the stable roof and even in at the open stable door! When the time came for me to show off this new accomplishment I threw the line with such vigour and accuracy that the astonished receiver, expecting it to fall short as usual, was nearly knocked overboard.

I rejoined Daphne in June, but this time I was to meet her at Gloucester, as she was doing a Sharpness trip with her brother, who had to leave her there. I remember I got a lift down the river in one of the tankers, which I thoroughly enjoyed, and on the way I offered some magazines to a quite young deck hand who refused them, saying he could neither read nor write. I was absolutely dumbfounded as I really thought there were only a very few, very old people left in some remote parts of the country who had had no schooling. I was as shocked as if he had said he were deaf and dumb. I managed to mumble something about how he must find it rather difficult at times, to which he cheerfully replied 'Oh well, wot yer never 'ad yer never misses, do yer?' This seemed a splendid philosophy and cheered me up a lot, especially later on when I was on the Grand Union, and found that illiteracy was quite usual.

We continued for the rest of the summer doing the usual trips—up to Tipton with the sacks of flour, back to Worcester with coal for the Mill and down to Sharpness for the grain. By now I knew much more about what I was doing and so was able to be quite helpful. We worked quite hard and we used to get furious when sometimes we saw half, even whole loaves of bread floating in the canal. It was somehow almost a personal insult—as if it had actually been made from some of the flour from those sacks over which we had sweated our guts.

On one occasion when we were at Townsend's Mill at Worcester, I dropped my gold wrist watch overboard. Strangely enough, at that time, it seemed quite a minor tragedy—I suppose because it was war-time and so many people were losing everything and anyway there was not the slightest chance that we would ever see it again. We optimistically tried raking for it, but the mud at that part of the canal must have been feet deep so we had no success. In the evening Denny Watton came over and we tried again, but it was quite hopeless. Several weeks later a dredger appeared on the scene and started to dredge opposite the mill, so with renewed hope I told the men the sad story and asked them to keep a look out. Needless to say everything imaginable was brought up except the watch. Sixteen months later a man who was fishing pulled up his line, and there it was caught on the hook! I imagine the tale of this extraordinary catch must have reached the ears of someone who remembered about my loss and the watch eventually got to Daphne who sent it on to me.

Unfortunately it was quite beyond repair but it was something even to have seen it again.

During one of our trips, on arrival at the top of Tardebigge locks we were rather surprised to find a boat tied up. She was a Shropshire Union narrow boat converted into a house-boat, and we were very impressed to see through one of the windows a beautiful bath. This was *Cressy*, owned by L. T. C. Rolt, who wrote the book *Narrow Boat*. Later on we got to know the Rolts very well; it was always nice having a talk with them, as the trip was really rather lonely. At that time we fraternised very little with the few boat people we met, and I used to feel that sometimes they considered we were working in opposition to them, as the *Heather Bell* was privately owned. Later on I learnt that it takes a very long time to be accepted on the water.

On the Worcester cut the rule of the road was to keep to the left when meeting other boats, which was rather awkward in the tunnels. The cabin chimney and the water can are always on the left of the cabin top, so it meant taking down the chimney and moving the can, otherwise they were likely to get damaged against the wall unless there was sufficient clearance. Many people have asked why we did not keep the can somewhere else, but the answer to that is that the can must be accessible to the steerer, who might be alone on the motor for many hours at a stretch. He might need to fill a kettle or get water for cooking during that time; also it was kept close to the chimney so that the two upright obstructions were together.

Most people are familiar with that charming habit some people have of spitting down on boats as they go under bridges. That, and throwing stones, lumps of earth or mud, is what the canal boater is likely to have to put up with whenever passing through a town. This used to madden Daphne: shouting at the children was no good, you always got back better than you gave, and in any event the culprits always had the advantage, as it is never

possible to get off the boat quickly enough to pursue them before
they have vanished. But at last she hit on a wonderful idea. We
would approach a bridge with a row of little boys with innocent
faces looking over at us. As the fore end of the boat started to go
through, one or two of them would lean right over, sucking in
their cheeks and collecting a good mouthful to aim at us as the
stern end went through, then Daphne would look up quite un-
suspectingly and call out 'What's the time?' The little boys,
completely taken aback and forgetting their intent, would hastily
gulp and yell out 'Don' know', or 'Har pars four', by which time
we were well out of range! A boatman once told me that when
they were going along by Paddington, his wife had handed up
his dinner to him to eat while steering, and he had just put it on
the slide in front of him, when down came a handful of horse
dung right in the middle of it. Those are the sort of things that
had to be put up with as all part of a boater's life.

Towards the end of the summer, Molly decided to leave the
Heather Bell; she had not been well and was going to take a shore
job for a time. However, she did not intend to leave the water for
good, and had been trying to work out a scheme whereby other
girls could be trained to become canal boat women so that more
boats would be available for transport. She had been to the
Ministry of War Transport, and they were showing great interest
in her ideas. At that time I could not imagine even being in
charge of a boat, let alone training anyone else, but Molly's idea
was that the three of us could go nearer London and start
training there. We discussed it a lot, but could not come to any
decision, so Molly left and Daphne and I carried on.

By the end of September, I had decided that I would leave
the *Heather Bell* at the end of the year. I was not sure if I wanted
to give up boating altogether or join in with the proposed training scheme, though it was still only at the discussion stage. So
apart from having made up my mind to leave, I was very un-

certain about what to do in the future. I did not know then that
at times likes that, you go on worrying and planning and trying
to come to a decision, but in the end events always seem to take
over, and, in spite of yourself, everything slips into place. This
was proved beyond a doubt a few months later when I literally
did not know what to do next. However, for the next few months
I would be carrying on with the *Heather Bell* and by now things
were running much more smoothly.

During October and November the trips continued and were
comparatively uneventful, then on 1 December we started off for
Sharpness on what turned out to be my last trip in the *Heather
Bell*. We let go at 11am and going down the Severn got a
snatch, which means that one of the empty boats overtaking us
gave us a tow, so we tied up in Gloucester Dock at 7.30. There
was a small French ship lying just ahead of us, and Daphne, who
speaks French fluently, got into conversation with one of the
sailors, and after supper we went on board and spent the evening
with them.

The next morning we were off early, and got down to Sharpness, loaded, and got away again by 3pm. It had been rather
foggy all day, and when we left it was getting quite thick, but
Daphne wanted to get to Gloucester and thought it would be all
right. I sheeted up the cargo as we were going along, and after
that went into the cabin and cut six rounds of bread and butter
ready for our tea, and got the kettle on. Suddenly I heard some
shouting, and got out to find we were meeting a pair of empty
tankers, and the man was calling out that there was another pair
close behind. It seemed only a few seconds, and they were coming out of the fog. I do not think they even saw or heard us, and
the next thing was a sickening crack as the poor *Heather Bell* was
caught in the bows. This swung the stern end round close to the
bank, so we were lucky enough to be able to jump off. It is difficult to remember exactly what happened, but the *Heather Bell*

was starting to settle down and the men from the tanker were very quick in getting ropes and tying her to the shore so that she didn't slip right down into the channel. I got one of the men to reach down into the fore-cabin which I was using and get out my handbag. As there was a good sized cut in the stem the cabin by then was full of water, and I remember him handing me the bag, which was the large variety, and open, rather like a bucket of water. The other cabin, where all our belongings were, was three parts under water, and all we had time to save was some of the bedding.

All this happened at 4.15pm, and when it was all over and the tankers had gone on there was nothing we could do, so we set off walking to the house of some people Daphne knew who lived nearby. I shall never forget that day: it is horrible seeing any kind of boat half sunk, and when she is yours it is a thousand times worse, far worse for Daphne as the *Heather Bell* really was her own.

The Butts, with whom we stayed, worked on the water, and Mr Butt was most kind and helpful. We slept that night on their sitting room floor, the whole family doing all they could for us, and the next day back we went to the scene of the disaster to meet various people who had to do with the salvage etc. We spent another night with the Butts, and then left for Worcester.

The salvaging was going to take several days, so Daphne let me go off to stay with my sister near London until she knew the extent of the damage to the *Heather Bell*, and if she would want me again. While I was away I went up to town and met Molly, who told me that the training scheme was really going to start, and that it would be on the Grand Union Canal. Apparently the Grand Union was the only carrying company willing to give the scheme a trial. At that time I was still very uncertain about what I wanted to do. I simply could not make up my mind whether to go on boating or join the WAAF, so in that state of mind we parted. Soon after that the *Heather Bell* was afloat again, and as she was to be towed up to Worcester for repairs Daphne asked me to go back and give her a hand. I rejoined her at Gloucester; back we went and I spent my last night on board in Diglis basin. The next morning I collected what few things were still left in the boat, said goodbye to the *Bounty* and then went up to the house to pack my clothes. Daphne and her mother had most kindly washed everything, which was no mean task, as they had all got thick with foul-smelling mud during the two and a half days they had been under water.

I left that afternoon, feeling rather shattered that it had all come to such a sudden end. For about the next three weeks I stayed with my mother or with my sister and I must have been unbearable, mooning about and not knowing what to do. Then at last, when with my sister, I decided to spend a whole day by the canal near Watford and not come back till my mind was made up. To help to get myself into the right mood I put on my old boat clothes and walked down to the canal at Cassiobury Park. As I walked along the tow path I met a lock keeper who asked if my boats were coming up which pleased me tremendously as it showed he took me for a real boatwoman! Little did I think I would meet him again, and that he was to become one of our best friends.

I continued along the path and eventually turned back for home, but still with no decision made. At the Cassiobury lock I sat on one of the checking stumps for some time, contemplating what seemed to me the vast size of the lock—after all it was twice as big as the single ones I had been used to—and then by a stroke of good fortune along came a pair of boats. They were empty and breasted up, which means they were closely tied together side by side. I stood watching them going lower and lower and looking down on to the beautifully swept and clean floor boards and that, I think, did it. I just couldn't clean up

Working boats: (*above*) approaching a lock that
has been made ready; (*below*) in the lay-by

Working boaters: (above) Mr Monk; (below) the Lewis Grantham family

after a cargo of coal any more, and not only one boat, but two. This of course was ridiculous as I would not be doing it all on my own, but I suppose I thought I would and that just settled it, my mind was made up: I had finished with the water and now for the WAAF.

The next day I went up to town to enlist, but on arrival was greeted with the news that all enlisting had stopped that very day! Funnily enough I was delighted; this was fine, there was no doubt now as to what I was to do, so I walked straight over the road to a telephone box and rang up the Grand Union. A meeting with Molly that afternoon; the next day down to the Grand Union depot at Southall, then over to the head office at Ruislip, and at last back home. Everything was now settled. Daphne was not coming with us, but staying where she was on the *Heather Bell*, and in the New Year Molly and I were to do a trip with a pair of boats worked by regular boat people, to learn the route and the management of a pair.

There was nothing to do now but wait.

D

Chapter 4

THE GRAND UNION

1942 STARTED with real winter weather, ice and snow, and not the kind which soon disappears. At the end of January, we were still waiting to join the Grand Union. We had written reminding them how anxious we were to start as soon as possible, but they had replied that all transport was being seriously affected by the severe weather conditions, and owing to other difficulties they were unable to say definitely when we could come. So that was that and there was nothing we could do about it.

I remember trying to find books to read on canal boating, but not with much success. At that time, very few people were interested in anything to do with canals, and what books there were on the subject did not tell us what we wanted to know—namely about the work and conditions of work from the point of view of someone with practical experience. The one exception was A. P. Herbert's *The Water Gypsies*, but it was not until we had had enough experience ourselves that we were fully able to appreciate the atmosphere and accuracy of all he wrote about canal life.

A whole week of February passed, and then at last the letter came. We were to report at Bulls Bridge depot on Monday 16 February. Bulls Bridge, Southall, was the head maintenance depot of the Grand Union Canal Carrying Company. There everything could be attended to in connection with the boats, equipment and engines.

The great day arrived and with two kit-bags containing my bedding and clothing, I started off. A van from the Grand Union met me at Southall station and drove me to the depot, Molly arriving soon after. We immediately went to the office to see Mr Wood, the works manager, who explained the difficulty they had had in finding a suitable couple who were willing to take us. They not only had to be good boaters, which of course includes being clean, but ones with no family so that Molly and I could have a cabin to ourselves. Mr and Mrs Albert Sibley filled the bill and had agreed to take us, but whether there was any eager enthusiasm on their part to do so was something we never did discover.

After discussing various matters, we were taken out to meet them; their boats, the *Edgeware* and *Purley*, were tied up outside the fitting shops. This was quite near the offices, but perhaps another reason why we were there was because they were away from all the other boaters. I rather think the publicity and embarrassment was more than the Sibleys could have borne had they had to receive these two unknown women trainees down in the lay-by. The lay-by was like a very large parking place for the boats and took about twenty pairs, lying side by side with the stern ends tied to rings on a concrete path. There the boats tied up while they were waiting for orders, for any repairs, illness, or perhaps even a confinement, and it was all very *intime*. 'Lay-by' was not then the familiar word that it is now and I remember how later on, one of our trainees thought it sounded like a biblical name, and that Ahab and Lay-by went well together!

The introductions over, Molly and I unpacked and got our things put away in the cabin of the motor boat, the *Edgeware*. The Sibleys lived in the butty boat, the *Purley*. With a pair of boats, the motor boat is always called the motor and the one which is towed is the butty. They are exactly the same size and length, but as the butty has no engine room, there is more cargo space and the cabin is slightly larger.

Inside our cabin were a few of the usual ornaments such as decorative brasses and some plates with openwork edges hanging beside the table-cupboard and stove. Apart from these, some oddments of line in one of the cupboards, and the hand bowl, the whole place was bare. The hand bowl was the only piece of movable equipment in the cabins supplied by the firm; it was strongly made and invaluable for all washing purposes. All such things as knobs, ornamental or otherwise, handles, bolts and catches belong to the temporary owners and are taken away when they leave the boat. Molly and I were going to cater for ourselves, so had brought only what was necessary in the way of crockery, a kettle, saucepan and frying pan, and we were allowed £1.50 a week each for our food and expenses.

The Sibleys were both wearing badges which impressed us very much; they were blue and white enamel with the badge and motto of the company in the centre and 'On national service' round the edge.

As we were to load at Brentford, we let go and went along to the top of the Norwood locks for the night. This was only a short distance from Bulls Bridge, but again I rather fancy the Sibleys wanted to get away from the depot. We both took turns at steering, and I know I found it rather difficult as the boats were tied side by side [breasted up], which causes a pull on the side of the butty and also both cratches were up (a cratch being a tent-like erection over a small section of the fore end of the cargo space). When the boats are empty, the motor boat remains lower by the stern owing to the weight of the engine, but the cratch seems to tower into the air and makes it impossible to see where you are going without standing on the gunwale and leaning out. However, Mr Sibley did not have to do this, so I supposed that in time we also should acquire what appeared to be a magical second sight.

The next morning, we let go at 7am, and as it was still quite dark, Mr Sibley took the tiller and Mrs Sibley and I went along the path to get the lock ready. On the Grand Union, this was called 'lock-wheeling', which seemed very strange after the 'hobbling' on the Worcester cut, also we kept to the right when meeting boats, which again was different from the Worcester and Birmingham. All the locks were broad, about 15ft, so the boats remained breasted up. Apart from the strangeness of broad locks after the narrow ones we had been used to before, there were also side ponds, which are small reservoirs of water at the side. By using the side pond paddles, water could be let out of the lock into the side pond or vice versa. This meant a saving of water, as otherwise to fill a lock, *all* the water had to be drawn off from the pound above, and there was no immediate means of replacing it.

While working these locks with Mrs Sibley, I asked her what we should call Mr Sibley—by that time the Mr and Mrs business had become rather tedious and somehow sounded all wrong—so when she said 'You call him Albert', that was one problem solved.

We were now beginning to meet a lot of horse-drawn barges coming up from Brentford, mostly carrying coal or timber. This caused a lot of delays as, owing to their size and weight, they were slow to move. There are different kinds of barges, but they are never less than 14ft beam. That of the canal narrow boat is roughly 7ft, so at last I realized the difference between boats and barges. At the fifth lock, Molly started to lock-wheel, so I joined Albert on the boats, and we continued like this until the eleventh, which is the last before the part of Brentford where we were loading.

I shall never forget the first time we tied up at Brentford. There were a lot of boats there, loading and waiting to load, and we knew that how we acquitted ourselves in front of them and the impression we gave was going to make a lot of difference, not only to ourselves, who were very much on trial, but also to the future of the training scheme. Albert winded the boats (turned them round) and we helped to tie up, while on every boat was at least one face looking and watching. Later on, we learnt that there was really nothing so devastating as the expression, or lack of expression, of a boater who does, or doesn't know you, or doesn't want to. However, later we acquired it too—quite immovable, absolutely silent, a look which sees nothing but takes in everything, and with not a flicker or sign of expression!

At last our turn came for loading; we were taking fifty tons of steel billets to Birmingham. The billets were almost 15ft long and eight at a time were lowered into the boat by a crane on the wharf. After loading 23 tons on the motor and 27 on the butty, we sheeted up. Though we were used to this, we found that Albert had a slightly different method of tying his side and top strings. All these strings were pulled as tight as wire, then firmly secured. When it came to unsheeting, they were all just as firm (except those we had done), yet with one upward tug they immediately loosened and untied, which made a great saving in time. When it was finished, the boats washed down and everything put in order, we retired to our respective cabins for a good clean up of ourselves, and as we were not going to let go till the morning, Albert said that later on we would all go to the pictures.

We got ourselves a meal of sorts and when the Sibleys were ready, we all set off along the path, past all the boats and the watching faces: the Sibleys trying to be unaware of their strange companions and we trying to be unaware that we were being sized up in no uncertain manner. On we went, and then suddenly, amongst all the dead pan faces, was one which smiled. This was wonderful, and to our great surprise, it turned out to be Dolly Griffiths from a Fellows Morton pair we often used to see when we were with the *Heather Bell*. Of course we stopped to chat, and she said she had heard one of us was drowned when we were run into on the Berkeley Ship and added 'We was ever so sorry as we felt we knew you, like'. Dear, dear Dolly, talking to us like that was the best thing possible and undoubtedly helped us to be accepted much sooner than if we had been completely unknown.

News travels fast on the cut, and in a most mysterious way, and no doubt by the next day, as far as Birmingham, it would be known that Albert had got two women trainees with him and, what was far more important to us, that they had both worked on the water before.

By the time we came out of the pictures, Albert had said we could call Mrs Sibley Ciss or Cissie, and although they invited us to call in at the pub with them on the way back, we decided to get back to the boats, as by then we were quite ready to turn in. Just as we were getting into bed, there was a knock on the cabin side and Albert handed in a pint of beer he had brought back from the pub. This was the first example of boaters' kindness and generosity and we dropped off to sleep after our first day on the Grand Union, tired and happy.

We made an early start the next morning in bitter cold, and took some time going up the locks owing to barges; however, Molly and I were lock-wheeling, so the exercise kept us warm and we had plenty of time for conversation with the lock-keepers, who were very friendly and helpful. Once clear of the locks, the boats were singled out, so now there had to be a steerer on each boat, and as we were in a long pound the butty was towed on the snubber. This snubber was about 70ft long, made of coconut fibre and when not in use was kept in the deck (fore end) of the butty. Albert explained that it made steering easier for both boats, as the butty was far enough behind to be unaffected by the wash from the propeller and the motor was well away from the weight of the tow. He also told us that later on, when we were working through the locks, the butty would be towed on either a short strap or on the towing rope. The short strap was just a short length of rope attached to the stud on the butty's deck, the other end with a loop on it was over the hook on the motor's counter. When entering a lock, the motor steerer took off the loop, and as the bows of the butty passed he placed it on the deck so that it could easily be picked up again when the lock was ready for the boats to leave. Naturally the motor's speed had to be adjusted as the butty took the strain, or the rope could easily be broken.

The towing rope method was more complicated, but it enabled the boats to leave a lock more quickly. A very long rope was supported by the raised mast and taken through running blocks right back to the hatches of the butty where it lay in coils on the cabin floor. As the motor left the lock with the butty in tow, her steerer paid out the rope, gradually taking the strain with a turn on an iron T stud screwed to the edge of the cabin top, the final check being made with a few more turns. The towing rope was always used with great care and caution as it was very easy for fingers or hands to get caught and crushed by the rapidly paying out rope, not to mention a leg getting caught up if some of the rope had been left in the hatches. It was never used if children were in the cabin as the danger from coils of rope whipping off the floor was far too great. Neither was it used in wet weather, which caused enough mess and inconvenience without the addition of wet rope in the cabin, and the T stud prevented the slide from being pulled over to keep out the rain.

When the boats were empty and it was not feasible for them to be breasted up, the butty was towed close up to the stern of the motor by two short lengths of rope on the butty stud, one end going over the hook and the other over the dolly on the motor counter.

As we were used to steering a motor, we stayed with Ciss on the butty and took turns there: Molly soon got used to it, but it took me some time. To begin with the position for steering was quite different; on the motor you stand on the counter, which remains very much the same level with the water when either loaded or empty. But now, the butty was deep down in the water and as the steerer stands in the hatches, the line of vision is from a very different angle. I also missed not having the engine, which could always be used to give just that little extra power to help you get round a corner, but now I had to depend on my own skill and judgement, and not having much of either, I often ran into trouble. However, Ciss, who was in the cabin most of the time getting on with the cooking, kept an eye on the view out at the rear, and according to what she saw could tell if it was necessary to leap up, seize the tiller and put things right. When Molly steered, I stayed in the cabin, and *vice versa*, so we both had plenty of time to take in every detail of the *décor*. Everything was spotlessly clean and so pretty and gay. Dividing the cabin were curtains with a valance, caught back with a bright ribbon, on the side bed a full-sized wireless set which took up a lot of room, but of course there was no such thing as a portable transistor in those days; framed photographs and plates were hung on the curtains and there was plenty of brass and crochet lace. Besides all the ornamental plates, there were brass rods over the stove, and a lot of very large brass knobs which had been taken from bedsteads. The stove, which looked as if it were never used, was like black satin and the ornamental parts highly polished silver. Just inside the cabin, high up on the left-hand side, was a small drawer called the ticket drawer, in which were generally kept the loading ticket and trip card, and round the bottom was a piece of crochet lace. We were simply fascinated with this cabin, but came to the conclusion that when we had our own, it would have to be considerably less ornamental until we knew a great deal more about running the boats and had mastered the art of being able to do at least three things all at the same time!

We tied up when we got back to Bulls Bridge, and after a talk with Mr Wood and one of the directors, we went back to Albert and Ciss and spent the evening with them. Everyone was rather doubtful whether we would be able to make the whole trip as the ice was very bad further on, but we felt that if anyone could get through, Albert would. In the morning, we went off to the labour exchange, and also got out emergency ration cards which were what all the boaters used, and then Ciss took us off to the shops. Before we let go in the afternoon, we were each given one of the badges, which I felt was just as good as getting a decoration.

That night, we tied up near the place where Albert's mum and dad lived, and we all went to see them. They were ex-boat people, and so friendly and kind. Their family of thirteen had all been born on the boats with the exception of the youngest.

By now, Ciss was calling Molly Molly, but she seemed to hesitate to call me Kit; however, once she had called me 'Missus', but Albert skilfully avoided any form of address. We were rather more pleased with ourselves too, as Ciss told us that we were a lot better than they had expected and that some of the boaters down at Brentford had said we were a good pair of girls for work.

Chapter 5

ICED UP

WE WERE wakened by Albert hammering on the side of the cabin and were away by seven. It was a good sharp frost, and we started off with the ice whistling and cracking as the motor went ahead. Lumps would break off and go sliding away on the unbroken ice in front, and all the time the crackling and whistling noise, which can be compared with nothing else.

We were soon at Cowley lock, the first of forty-five climbing steadily up to Tring summit.

Albert took the motor in on the right, took off the towing rope from the hook on the stern, and neatly threw it over the butty's cratch as she glided in on the left. He then jumped up on the cabin top, sprang up the wall on to the side of the lock and shut the gate behind the motor. Meanwhile Ciss, holding the end of a rope attached to the side of the butty, stepped off on to the side, ran up the steps, took a quick turn round a checking stump, and steadied the butty so that she didn't run in too fast and bump the cill at the other end. Then equally quickly and neatly, she unwound the rope from the stump and tied it firmly to another one further on. This was to prevent the butty from washing back against the bottom gate, as the water rushed in when the top paddles were drawn. She then shut the bottom gate and immediately Albert was winding up the top paddles and the lock was filling. This all took about a minute, and of course being done so efficiently by skilled boat people appeared the simplest thing in the world. However, our turn was to come. Not only would we have to master this new technique of taking a pair of boats through broad locks, but we would have to teach others to do it too.

Cowley is a gauging lock, so after Albert had taken the trip card in to the office to have the date entered on it, out came the man to take the draught of each boat. The gauging of the boats was an accurate method of checking the tonnage carried, on which dues were paid.

This gauging was done by a gauging rod, a tube of copper about 7ft long for loaded boats or a rather shorter one for when they were empty. About 2ft from the top of the rod was the crutch, which rested on the gunwale when the rod was placed in the water. Inside the tube was a measuring stick with a float on the bottom which forced the measure out of the top of the rod and according to the figures shown, the necessary calculations were made. Each boat was gauged at four places along each side. There were four gauging points on the canal between Regent's Canal Dock, where the Grand Union joined the Thames, and Birmingham or the Coventry Canal: Paddington, Cowley, Hillmorton, near Rugby, and Sutton Stop which was really Hawkesbury, near Coventry, but known as Sutton Stop after a family who were toll keepers there in Victorian times.

During the gauging both water cans were being filled at the tap by the lock side, and we were now ready to go on, but one more thing had to be done which was new to us. Cowley lock always had to be left empty, ready for uphill traffic, so Molly and

I were left on the path. Out went the motor, Albert picked up the towing rope (or strap, as we had now learnt all ropes were called), attached it to the hook on the motor's counter and then, as the butty cleared the top gates, we shut them, dropped the paddles and raced to the bottom end to draw the other ones. We then ran along the path and were able to step on to the boats as they passed under the bridge. We were very thankful that this was the only lock where this had to be done.

The next pound was a long one, so it was not until the third bridge that we had to get off to lock-wheel. From then on, it was necessary to have someone out on the path going ahead the whole time. Neither of the Sibleys' bicycles was in working order, so we just had to walk. The day wore on and we wore out, pounding round the locks, drawing up the paddles and trudging on to the next. Of course we did get back to the boats every now and then for a short spell, but Albert was naturally taking full advantage and making the most of having two good mates to do the lock-wheeling, so that he could press on as far and as fast as possible. We were having what is called a 'bad road', which meant that every lock we came to was against us, and eventually we caught up with the pair which was causing this—Albert's brother Tom.

By then we had passed Uxbridge, Rickmansworth and Croxley Green and were now in Cassiobury Park— one of the prettiest parts of the canal and where I had walked when trying to make up my mind about my future. While we were in the first of the two locks, along came the same lock-keeper who had spoken to me. He, also, was called Albert, and the locks were always known as Albert's Two. Just after the locks were some of the most vicious corners imaginable and these too were referred to as Albert's Bends. *Our* Albert on the motor and Ciss in the butty steered round them with the greatest of ease, but Molly and I wondered if it would be as easy as that when the time came for us to try!

At King's Langley, we passed the Ovaltine factory. Ovaltine had their own boats which were dazzlingly clean and beautifully painted. Several of them were tied up, some unloading, and others waiting to unload their coal. The sun shining on all the roses, castles, gaily painted tillers and gleaming brasses looked really splendid.

All this time, the canal was running parallel with the railway on the right and the road on the left. The trains roared and rattled past on the line, the traffic hummed away on the road and we slogged slowly along in the middle. Very soon, we were working through the five locks called the New 'Uns—a strange name, as they had been made many years ago when the original course of the canal had been altered for the convenience of Dickinson's paper mills, so the two locks at Nash and the three at Apsley became the New 'Uns and undoubtedly the New 'Uns they will remain.

Still we went on and still more locks, and now the ice was beginning to get bad again. This delayed us a lot as it packed up behind lock gates and prevented them from opening flush with the walls. Sometimes, great lumps of ice, inches thick, would pile up on each other and, until they were removed, the boats could not get in, so then we learnt what ice podging was. For this, a very long pole with iron prongs on the end is used, thrust down hard enough to allow some of the pieces underneath to go deeper and release themselves; then those on the surface could be floated away. All this thrusting and pushing had to be done so many times that our arm muscles got almost paralysed with lifting the pole, which seemed to get heavier and heavier. However, it was something to have learnt how to deal with this problem which we were certain to meet again before the war was over, and when we were out on our own with no Ciss and Albert to do most of the work.

Eventually we tied up near Berkhamsted station about 7pm

just behind the other Sibleys' boats. I then recall we rushed off to the fish shop with Ciss, but after waiting 20 minutes we got only chips, which was a great disappointment. Before going to bed, Albert informed us that tomorrow we should be getting into the really bad ice and he didn't think we should get far.

The next morning we did not let go till eight. The ice was terrible and it took us till 11.30 to get through the next six locks. It was worse for the Tom Sibleys going in front, and they had to have a horse on the path helping to pull them through. Then it started to snow, which made everything look very pretty but didn't make things any easier, but at last we got to the Cowroast lock. We had been climbing steadily since leaving the depot at Bulls Bridge and had been through 45 locks, but here we were on Tring summit and the next locks we came to would be downhill.

Now it was a question of just going on till further progress was impossible, which could not be far ahead. Albert knew there was nothing else behind, also that everything coming our way was ice-bound, so soon after we left the lock he stopped the boats—we did not bother to tie up—and had our dinners. I remember the exact spot where we did this, and how iron-grey, hard and cold everything looked as we sat in our warm cabin eating our food. I often used to picture the scene on other trips, particularly in the summer if it happened to be so hot that you could hardly bear it.

Tring summit is about three miles long with high banks on either side, covered with trees and bushes. It was quite sheltered from the wind, and with the gently falling snow it all looked rather like a stage set. At one point, great woody tendrils were hanging down from a great height on some of the trees. We wondered what it could be as it looked strong enough to swing on. In the summer, we discovered it was what must have been the oldest Old Man's Beard.

Out of the shelter of Tring summit we met the wind which was piercingly cold and as the ice was very bad Albert decided we would soon have to tie up. We struggled down the Marsworth locks and not long after, at 4.30, we tied up.

Just ahead of us were the Tom Sibleys and by now we had got to know them all—Lena, the wife, Albert aged 13, and Georgie who was 10. Their eldest son, Tommy, who was 21, had just got married, and his boats were iced up further on at Fenny Stratford. Later on, he arrived by bicycle along the towing path, having come to see how far his father had got, as he knew he was due to be coming that way.

After supper he, Tom, Albert and young Albert all came into our cabin. This was really our first experience of hearing boaters talking together. What tales we heard, and what questions we asked! Altogether it was a grand evening, and we went to bed with our heads full of tales of snubbers on the blades, boats on the cill, Hatton 21 and a thousand other things which had all been most bewildering; but amongst other things, we learnt that Berkhampsted was always called Berka, Rickmansworth Ricky, and that we were on our way to 'Burningham', 'Brumigum' or 'Brum'.

During the night we thought it seemed a bit colder, and when we looked out in the morning, our boats were frozen in. Where it had been clear water before, the ice was a good half-inch thick. Ahead of us it was quite solid; all the great lumps piled up on each other and frozen over.

We soon had the fire going and then had our breakfast. After that, Albert and Tom started up their motors to see if there was any chance of breaking a way through. It proved quite hopeless, so now we knew we were properly iced up and this would be our place of residence until an ice-breaker got through or a thaw set in.

It was Sunday, but on the chance of finding some small shop

open, we walked to Ivinghoe, about a mile along the road, and got some bread. Soon after we got back, what should appear down the road, on a bicycle, but one of those ubiquitous Indians complete with bulging suitcase balanced on the handlebars. These Indians were to be seen before the war in isolated districts of the British Isles—I even saw one in Inverness being ferried across to the Black Isle and it is odd to remember that those were the days when the sight of a coloured person was not only unusual, but had a certain air of mystery. This one, who appeared so unexpectedly on that bitter Sunday morning, must have thought that here was a chance of doing business, so he came across the hard frozen meadow towards us. Ciss and Albert stood leaning over the hatches and not attempting to go and inspect his wares, but they graciously consented to him coming over the plank which reached from the shore to the cabin top. This he did, and then proceeded to open the case. What a strange picture it was, there on the cabin top, the crouching Indian, dressed in a brown overcoat, khaki trousers and a not too clean silk turban, holding up sky-blue lock-knit bloomers, scarves and handkerchiefs before his anything but eager customers, and all around the snow and ice.

We were iced up for ten days and never once do I remember being bored or not having anything to do. We looked out of our cabin down the canal to a very pretty bridge at the side of which was a huge elm tree, stark and bare, and away to the left was Ivinghoe beacon. Our cabin was snug and warm; when we were outside we wore plenty of clothes, and as we were always well occupied, that kept our circulation going. Every day we went across to the farm to get the drinking water and collect our letters, and nearly every day walked to Ivinghoe for the bread.

One day, Albert fixed up a line and Ciss had a big wash, so we joined in too, rinsing most of our things in a hole in the ice. Other days we went on wooding expeditions, as the coal situation was

E

getting a little delicate. However, one of the company's vans
brought us a supply of coal before we were right out.

We liked Albert and Georgie very much and had some good
fun together. They came into our cabin at least once a day, and
we played all sorts of games. 'I Spy' was rather hard on Georgie,
though, as he could not read or write, but he was by no means
put off by this handicap, being very intelligent and quick. Albert
had learnt the alphabet and could write his name, but he was
three years older than Georgie and had had more opportunity of
going to the boat children's school at Bulls Bridge.

This school was held in a converted wide boat which had once
been afloat but was now 'moored' on the shore. The teacher was
faced with very great difficulties as the ages of her pupils varied
considerably and their attendance was naturally very irregular,
as sometimes their boats might be in the lay-by for a week, or
even longer, but more often it was only for a day or two.

There was a school at Brentford, and I believe one in Birmingham, which they could also attend, but after a few days they
would be off again and it might be weeks before they had another
opportunity of schooling.

The Sibleys told us that sometimes the children stayed with
their grandparents so that they could have a regular education,
spending the holidays with their parents on the boats, but this
did not happen very often as the parents preferred to keep them
on the boats all the time, and in any event it was not always
possible for the grandparents to have them.

One afternoon, we took both the boys in to the pictures at
Tring; this was a great success, and when we came out, of all
extraordinary things, ice-creams were being sold at the door, so
of course the boys spotted this and lingered behind. It was freezing hard, and as Molly and I walked along in the snow and bright
moonlight, up they dashed, thrust a whole 4d tub into our hands,
and said 'There yer are—there's one between the two of yer'.

This was really a true gift, as I know it would never have entered their heads that we should refuse. Nearly always, we spent the evenings all together in one or other of the cabins. This meant six grown-ups and two children, but we all packed in somehow, and thoroughly enjoyed ourselves.

We often used to picture our friends and relations suffering the discomforts of being iced up in a house—huddled round the fire in a draughty room; putting up with all the inconvenience of frozen and burst pipes; creeping along cold passages and going to bed in icy bedrooms. We used to feel quite sorry for them. Here we were in our tiny cabin, and every night we enjoyed the luxury of going to bed with a 'fire in the bedroom'.

Chapter 6

TO THE COVENTRY FOR COAL

THE THIRD of March was brilliantly sunny, with a good strong breeze, and soon after breakfast along came the ice breaker, churning up enormous slabs of ice, which were much thicker than we expected after all the sunshine. The ice breaking was done by a maintenance tug—often called a tunnel tug because they had once been used to tow the horse-drawn boats through the tunnels after the days when they were 'legged' through by men. Previous to the tug being used we were told that ice breaking was done by a boat with a raised bar fixed along the centre from stem to stern. This bar was held by a team of men standing on either side who vigorously rocked the boat and as the ice broke up the boat was slowly towed forward from the path by horses—six to twenty or more.

Thanks to the more up-to-date method we got away at about 11am, Molly and I lock-wheeling of course, but though the ice was broken we took a very long time getting through the locks and only got as far as Leighton Buzzard, where we did some shopping and then, as usual, all went off to the pictures.

Half an hour after we had let go the next morning it started to rain, and it rained from 6.30am till 5.30pm, a steady downpour. Molly and I togged ourselves out in oilskins and sou'-westers, but Albert just put on an old overcoat and Ciss put up her umbrella while steering the butty. I remember thinking how sensible we were to have the right waterproof clothing and that something should be done to supply the boatmen with oilskins, but after we were a bit older and wiser we realised that the boatman, as usual, was no fool and there was always a good reason for what he did. Admittedly, the coat got wetter and wetter, but the wet soaked in and it was not until it was completely saturated that he was forced to tie up and it was then hung up in the engine room to dry. With the oilskins, the water just ran off, straight into your shoes, soaking your trousers and making a nasty mess in the cabin which all had to be cleaned up. A long oilskin, too, was an awful nuisance when crossing over lock gates, so we cut them short, but this meant having to get waterproof leggings—something else which had to be stowed away when not in use, and something else to dig out and put on when time was such an important factor. Had oilskins been issued to the boaters, I very much doubt that they would ever have been used for the purpose for which they were intended!

But whoever we were and whatever we wore, we all felt the same about rain, especially when it was a day of working through locks. Luckily, on this soaking day, the locks were few and far between and after a brief stop at the one at Fenny Stratford, where rations could be bought at the Red Lion, we were off on the first really long pound, and again the butty was towed on the snubber.

We progressed in this manner for about three and a half hours and despite the rain, enjoyed the peace and quiet of the butty. Before, when we had been near enough to the motor, we got a lot of noise from the engine, but here we were, gliding along drawn apparently by an invisible force and with nothing to do but steer—or so we thought!

In reality, contrary to appearance, there is always *someone* who is pretty busy catching up with all the things which could not be done while working through the locks. We once met the Jack Wilsons in a long pound, and Mrs, who was alone on the butty, had a sewing machine on the cabin top in front of her and while steering with the tiller tucked under her left arm, she was busily machining away at some curtains!

Not long before the end of this pound, we crossed a small aqueduct which Albert referred to as the Pig Trough. It was not much wider than the boat with the tow path on one side and on the other, a very small parapet with a drop of about 30ft to the river below. This was our first experience of an 'ackiduck' (it was in fact Wolverton iron trough aquaduct over the Great Ouse) and I remember hoping the boat would not bump into the side, which I felt certain would give way and we would all go crashing down below.

During the trip we often noticed that there was a small concrete stump on the bank a short distance from a lock and Albert explained that it marked the distance from the lock inside which the approaching boats had the right of way. It was also to stop another pair from overtaking those already within lock distance. Naturally there was nothing to enforce this rule, and many a good fight had taken place between lock-wheelers arriving at the same lock and each insisting that their boat had the right of way. Paddles would be drawn by one man and immediately dropped by the other, sometimes all drawn at the same time, and to the accompaniment of swearing and shouting followed by a good hand to hand. Meanwhile both pairs of boats would be kept waiting until one or the other could land reinforcements and gain the victory.

Every day produced some new experience, apart from the fact that every day we were on a different part of the canal. We tried to memorise landmarks, especially if they came before some special feature like a bad bend, the approach of locks, even a fresh water tap, as drinking water supplies were often few and far between. We were also trying to get used to handling a pair of boats, but this was not easy, as Albert, quite naturally, did not want to waste precious time by letting us take them very often. After all, the boatman was paid on freights, not by the week, so the quicker he did the trip, the sooner he drew his pay, though he was generally allowed a certain amount of starting money.

The boaters worked long hours and wasted no time once they were on the move as often, through no fault of their own, they could be held up and delayed: perhaps a lock closed for repairs, engine trouble, having to stop and clear something off the propeller shaft, or a delay waiting to load or unload. Their starting money varied, but however much it was meant that much less in the pay packet at the end of the trip. Besides not wanting to lose more time than was necessary, a boater was not used to imparting his knowledge. He was a boater born and bred, born on a working boat and had grown up in working boats, so there was never a time when he didn't know all about their management. This made it impossible for him to imagine what it was like for a grown person to start from scratch and try to learn what he, the boatman, had never been aware of learning. I know I was truly thankful to have had even that one year with the *Heather Bell*, without which everything would have been doubly difficult.

Despite the length and general bewilderment of that first trip on the Grand Union, there were certain landmarks which made an instant and permanent imprint on our memories. One of these was the unusual grey stone bridge just after the lock at Cosgrove—another, the weather-beaten, beautiful colours of the pub sign at the Lord Nelson at Braunston. On later trips, when

we were out on our own, landmarks were generally graven on our memories owing to some disastrous happening like the snubber on the blades, someone falling in or a worse than usual stemming up!

But getting used to this London-Birmingham-Coventry-London trip was going to take a long time and it seemed almost impossible that one day we would actually know what was round the next corner, how long it would take to get from A to B and where we would be tying up for the night.

The next locks we came to after Wolverton aqueduct were the seven uphill at Stoke Bruerne, so the greater part of the long snubber had to be pulled in on to the butty deck, and a turn taken round the stud, leaving a sufficient length for Albert to use while working through them. He explained that once through the top lock we would be in another long pound, so the full length of the snubber would be needed again.

On arrival at the top lock, we learnt from Ciss that it was a great landmark for the boaters as it was here that Sister Mary lived—Sister Mary being the nurse employed by the Grand Union to see after the health of the boat people. Her house was right on the lock side, and on that day there were three pairs of boats tied up along the tow path and Ciss was able to tell us exactly why and all about them. On one, someone was due to have a baby; in another, someone had a bad leg which needed frequent dressings; and the third was locked up as the boatman had had to go to hospital and his wife had gone to stay with her parents. We gathered that this Sister Mary was a great character and that the boaters thought the world of her. She apparently knew them all, and a lot of their mums and dads before them, so she had their complete confidence and trust.

We just had time to take in all the charm of this lock, the attractive old buildings on one side, some of which had at one time been used as a rope walk, the *Boat* pub opposite, the row of magnificent poplar trees, and we were away, once more on the full length of the snubber.

Albert had already tested and switched on the head-lamp on the motor and Cis had lit a little miniature hurricane lamp which she hung on the butty tiller as a rear light so that all was ready for Blisworth tunnel, now not far ahead.

Both boats were supplied with quite powerful electric head-lamps, but they had to be shaded to comply with the black-out regulations, even more so than car head-lamps owing to the reflection from the water, and by the time the dimming down was approved by the Ministry officials it was not much help to the steerer. It did not bother the boatman though, as he knew the cut like the back of his hand and could quite well manage without. In the event of the electric light being out of action when going through a tunnel, a regulation masthead oil lamp was used. These were provided by the company and invariably the boaters painted them with the same designs as all their other equipment.

We had already been told by Albert that there were five ventilation shafts in Blisworth tunnel. To make the tunnel nineteen shafts were sunk so that men could tunnel out in two directions joining with similar excavations from the other shafts. All the soil dug out was hauled to the surface and the large mounds made by it can be seen to this day. All the shafts were eventually filled in except for the five, and when looking up them they appear like very large chimney stacks, except that drips and little cascades of water are continually coming down, which the boater takes care to avoid. When taking the road over the top they look like squat chimneys, but sufficiently high to prevent the possibility of any accident.

We had had experience of tunnels on the Worcester & Birmingham cut, but this one was rather different. For one thing, it was much longer, nearly two miles, and of course we had never been through one with a butty in tow. We rounded the next bend and there it was—the black hole in the side of the hill with its great brick surround, the entrance to Blisworth tunnel, opened in 1805 and still going strong. In went the motor leaving us gliding along in silence and then we were in. At once we were struck by the noise and rumbling throb of the engine echoing all around us which put a stop to any light conversation and this continued for about thirty-five minutes, till the motor emerged from the other end, when suddenly everything was quiet again, except for the lap flap of the water, and then out we came.

It was nearly eight when we tied up that night at Heyford. We had been on the go for fourteen hours, and I think Albert felt we 'learners' had had enough. If he and Ciss had been on their own, I expect they would have carried on until the bottom of the next locks; however, they didn't, and we were thankful to turn in.

When we looked out the next morning, to our amazement everything was once again covered in snow and perilously slippery. I suppose we thought we had finished with all that, but little did we know we were to have a great deal more before we got back to the depot. That first trip was certainly one of new experiences in more ways than one.

Another whole day of snow, ice and more locks to contend with, the first being the seven at Buckby—always pronounced Bugby. At one of them, we were joined by Ciss's old dad, a retired boatman of seventy-plus, who took charge of the butty while Ciss went along to see her mum in their cottage on the tow path, and we, of course, went on lock-wheeling. We were amazed to see the way this old man handled the boat; such calm, unhurried efficiency, in fact the expert, and the exact opposite of my over-eager hurrying, chattering and scampering. We left him at the top lock and Ciss rejoined us, carrying a pile of clean washing which her mum had done for her.

A little further on, we were at Norton Junction Toll Office

where the canal branched right for Leicester. A brief stop while Albert had the trip card marked and then we were off again heading for Braunston. Quite soon, we were at Braunston tunnel, not quite so long as the one at Blisworth, but peculiar because it was not dead straight. In fact, at one point, if you were steering the boat close to the side, the opening at the other end appeared as a half moon of light owing to the curve of the wall. Albert told us that if you met another boat on this bend, you could get jammed, but nothing happened to us and a few minutes after leaving the other end we came to the six downhill locks. These were not nearly so deep as some, particularly those at Stoke and Buckby and in consequence the paddles were not so hard to draw. Molly and I lock-wheeled and thoroughly enjoyed them despite the fact that it was snowing hard all the time.

As the last two were ready, we asked Albert if we could go on ahead to Nurser's Boatyard to see if Daphne and the *Heather Bell* were still there, as we knew she had been taken to Braunston after being sunk. Off we went and found her in the dry dock, looking very smart, having been completely repainted, and there in the cabin were Daphne and her mother. They were waiting for the ice to clear so that they could get back to Worcester. We could only stay a few moments as we had to dash off and pick up our boats at a bridge, which we managed to do, having timed it perfectly.

Shortly after the boatyard, the canal again branched left and right—left for Oxford and Brum and right for Coventry and the coalfields. We passed quite twenty pairs tied up waiting to get through to Coventry as much of that part of the canal was still frozen over. However, we were taking the left arm and off we went, again on the long snubber as there were no more locks until we had turned off on to the Warwick & Napton canal at Napton Junction. Albert told us that all the next locks—fifty-one of them—were the 'New Design'. New, because after the Grand Union

Canal Co was formed in 1929, they decided to carry out a scheme on this stretch of canal for replacing the single locks with wide ones, the work being started in 1932. I can't say I liked these 'New Design' at all to begin with. Having worked through so many of the old kind by this time, I was quite used to them, but now, instead of drawing the paddles on the gates and being able to see the ratchet rise, there were no gate paddles at all, but both top and bottom paddles were on the lock side and encased in iron. This meant that you couldn't see if the paddle was up or down, unless you looked through a small hole in the casing. These locks were deeper too, so needing more turns of the windlass to get the paddles up, and as the balance beams were made of iron instead of wood, they were much heavier to pull open or shut. However, they were a lot cleaner to work as all the lock surround was concrete, and nice little ridges had been made to put your feet against when tugging at the gates. All locks had these ridges, but between them was generally rough ground which in winter became mud and pools of water.

We worked through twenty-three of these locks, and here we had our first experience of a staircase lock—two locks which only have three pairs of gates, as there is no pound between: the middle pair acting as the top gates of one, as well as the bottom gates of the other. Naturally this means they are twice the height of the other gates and it is quite an experience the first time you look up at them from a boat in the empty lock below. After Wigrams 3 came Itchington 10, Radford 10* and then we were in the Leamington pound, eventually tying up outside the gasworks at about 7.30pm. This was a favourite tie up of the Sibleys, as there was a fish shop very near. We were much more aware of

---

* These are the names as I knew them. Now they are usually called Calcutt 3, Stockton 9, Itchington Bottom, Bascote 4, Welsh Road, Wood, Fosse 3 and Radford.

the gasworks, which were pretty smelly, and the neighbourhood along the two paths was not at all like what I remembered of Leamington Spa. I had been there before the war at a time when there was a health exhibition and where, amongst the exhibits on the Public Health Department stand, was a bed-bug taken from some slum clearance area, and I remember passing it by with a superior and disinterested glance, little thinking that before my next visit I would be on very familiar terms with them, and would enter the town via its gasworks and very un-Spa-like neighbourhood with my face covered with a crop of bed-bug bites.

Bugs in the boats were not unusual and could appear in the most immaculate cabins. I must have had my butty boat for well over a year and then, suddenly, in the middle of a trip, they appeared. There was nothing we could do about it, so we just had to put up with them until we got back to the depot. Once there, we could be 'stoved out'. This meant that a lighted formalin candle was put in the cabin and all cracks round the doors and any opening completely sealed. It worked quite well and afterwards the dead bugs could be swept up. Some of the boaters were not as clean as others, and it was not so simple for the ones that had bugs to get their cabin stoved, as it meant clearing out all the food, themselves and the children for several hours. Quite apart from the problem of where to go in the meantime, the waiting might also prevent them from getting some good order for loading, so often they just put up with them. If we ever visited boats where we suspected bugs, we always took care to sit on the step or coal box where it was less likely that they would get on our clothes and be taken back to our own cabins.

The next morning, after the two Warwick locks, we had our introduction to Hatton, a flight of twenty-one. We heard a lot about them, as every boater had delighted in telling us how hard they were. They proved to be all and more than we had been told. By the time we had reached the eleventh I was already tired and there before us, stretching up over the hillside, were six more, much closer together and from the distance looking rather like giants' tombstones. On we went, round the bend and then we could see the top. Only three more, but they proved to be harder than any of the others. Once through the top lock, it was a great relief to put down the windlass and start off on an eight-mile pound which gave time to recover.

Albert cheered us up by telling us there were only five more of these locks, then a ten-mile pound, and we would be at Tyseley Wharf, Birmingham, where we were to unload.

When we eventually reached these locks at Knowle, we found the ice on them was even worse. The grease on the paddles had frozen, making them stiffer and harder to wind. It took us a long time to get them up, but at last we were through and off on the last lap to Tyseley where we tied up at about eight.

There seemed to be dozens of boats already there, but Albert explained that this was because many parts of the canal were still frozen and they were waiting to be able to get away. Once again, we were a source of great interest, but being under the wing of the Sibleys acted as a kind of passport.

We unloaded in the morning, after getting both boats unsheeted. There had been another sharp frost in the night and the top cloths were frozen stiff, also all the strings, but they were not so unpleasant to handle as one would imagine. Needless to say, there was nothing that we did, or did not do, that was missed by any of our watching neighbours.

The afternoon was spent cleaning up the bottom of the boats and all the brasses, which were in a filthy state after all the rain and snow, and in the evening we went into the butty cabin and had a good session with Ciss and Albert. They told us that when we let go in the morning, we would be going back the way we had come as far as Braunston, and then on to Coventry to get orders for the coal we would be taking back to London. They

Boat females: (*above*) trainees entering a lock watched by Kit on the left; (*left*) canal cats; (*right*) Mrs Skinner

Narrow boats: (*above*) part of Mrs Hannah Ward's cabin; (*below*) a Samuel Barlow butty

also told us there was another way to Coventry via Fazeley, which they referred to as The Bottom Road, and which we gathered they all hated. Eventually the time came, owing to a water shortage, when we all had to go the bottom road, so we were able to see for ourselves. The first locks were the six at Camp Hill—

....*19*........

To M.The..Key..Glass..Works,..Ltd•....

Received from THE GRIFF COLLIERY COMPANY, LTD., per

Steerer...Miss..Garford•.......................................

Boats Battersea & Pavo•..............................

.................2......*Loads of Coal.*

(*Signed*), ...

which were not far from Tyseley, and they were followed by the Saltley five. The surroundings were extremely unattractive, filthy water, dreary factories on either side, and as all the locks were narrow the boats had to work independently, the butty being bow-hauled, that is, towed by hand. This was very unpleasant as we had to use the cotton line which naturally got wet, and as it was not always possible to keep it from dragging on the towpath which was made of cinder dust, it, the boats, and ourselves were far from clean, or sweet-tempered, by the time we had worked down to the bottom. It was a relief when we got out into the

F

country, but even then it was not very nice as it was so desolate
and lonely, apart from the hard work of the narrow locks. As long
as I was training other girls I never liked taking them round the
bottom road and having to show them a completely new technique of handling the boats, when by the time we had got to
Tyseley they had just begun to get used to what would be their
usual route.

However, that was all in the future and at the moment we had
quite enough to bother about. We would be sent to any one of
the loading places—Griff, Pooley Hall, Longford, Newdigate or
Atherstone and the coal might have to be taken back as far as the
A.B.C. bakery at Camden Town, but they hoped it would be a
shorter run to one of the Dickinson paper mills at Nash, Apsley
or Croxley. More and more names to remember and how long
would it be before they became places to us, and not just names?

Amongst the boats which were leaving the next morning were
friends of Ciss and Albert called Pearsall; Tom, Carrie his wife,
Rose, Lily, Tommy, and the mate, a girl who, Albert told us,
was one of a family of seventeen. So Albert and Tom arranged
that we should butty them, which meant that we would follow
them the whole time, tie up with them and start off with them
again in the morning. Also, when boats butty each other, the first
pair, after going through a lock, will generally close the gates and
draw a paddle so that it is partly ready by the time the other pair
comes along.

Off we went, and as the boats were now empty, the butty was
towed by two very short towing straps so that her fore-end was
held close to the stern of the motor, and therefore she needed no
steering. This was very convenient when you wanted to get from
the butty to the motor, as you only had to walk along the top
planks, step round the cratch on to the deck and jump down on
the counter of the motor. When loaded, it was not so simple.
You either had to ease the motor down to allow the butty to come

close enough to be able to jump across, or you had to get off at a bridge, walk along the path to the next bridge, wait for the motor to come along and then get on.

When we reached the top of Knowle locks, the ice was terrible. There was no hope of the motor being able to pull the butty through, so from the bridge up to the lock we had to bow-haul her—Carry, Rosie, Bee, Molly, Ciss and me on the end of a cotton line pulling for all we were worth. To make things harder, there was quite deep snow on the towpath which got very slippery as we trod it down. We took a long time to work through the locks, but it would have taken very much longer if we had not been with the other pair of boats and had all the extra help. But apart from that, we were going back the way we came, which made a tremendous difference compared with the previous six days when we were seeing every lock and part of the canal for the first time.

To have taken six days, not counting being iced up, from the depot at Bulls Bridge to Tyseley was unheard of for the boaters, who generally averaged 4-4½ days when conditions were normal. However, on looking back, the bad weather was really to our advantage. Being slowed down meant that we had breathing space and more time to take things in, and though the ice made work conditions so much harder, it was much less hard than had we been on our own, and as we were sure to experience a hard winter again in the future, we did at least know what to expect and how to deal with it.

By the time we reached Hatton, it was brilliant sunshine, the first we had seen for days; everything looked light and bright and we felt the same, so we practically scampered down the twenty-one locks, or so it seemed, compared with the hard drag up them in the freezing cold only a few days before.

We were through the rest of the New Design locks the following day, and when we were back on the Oxford heading for

Braunston, we met the *Heather Bell* chugging along through the ploughed-up ice on her way back to Worcester. She looked splendid with all her bright new paint, but we only had time to shout a few words of admiration as we passed. At Braunston we found the ice breaker had just got through from Coventry, so that stretch of the canal was now open. It was lucky we arrived when we did, as the first pair of the cavalcade which had been ice-bound was only just ahead as we came round the bend. From now on we were once again covering new ground—or water—as we had again branched left at the junction where previously we had also branched left for Birmingham. This junction was easy to recognise as there was a small triangular island—the only one on the whole of the route—so we had only to remember to bear left from whichever direction it was approached.

Life was now easy the whole way to Hawkesbury with the exception of the three locks at Hillmorton. These were narrow, and in pairs, so that the motor used one while the butty used the other.

We made Hawkesbury that night and tied up at 8.30. It was too dark to see much of the surroundings, but after a good wash and tidy up, we all went across to the Greyhound. This was really our first good session in a boaters' pub. During the trip we had not always tied up near one, and when we had, we were sometimes too exhausted to join in, but felt more like staying in the cabin and mulling over all the happenings of the day. The Greyhound was right on the canal side; it was a great centre for the boaters and you could always be sure of meeting people there who were connected in some way with the canals. We turned in that night feeling that, strange outsiders that we were, Ciss and Albert had accepted us and that we really were beginning to be part of the boating world.

On looking out of the cabin the next morning, we saw a lot of steerers hanging about and kicking their heels outside the office waiting for their orders. Every now and then, out came one with a slip of paper and with a brief word or two to the others, went straight back to his boats, sometimes converging with his wife who had been out doing the shopping; then, without any delay, they were off.

The night before, we had heard Albert and Tom speculating as to what orders they were likely to get. The same strange names were bandied about, one of which we would be heading for in the morning.

Tom Pearsall got his orders first, for Longford; this pleased him as it was not only the nearest, but the method of loading was the quickest, so he would soon be on his way back to London. But Albert was to go to Baddesley which was some distance away and more locks to go through, so with next to no delay the engine was started and we were off.

Hawkesbury, or Sutton Stop as it was more often called by the boaters, is the end of the Oxford Canal. For the last hundred yards or so it runs parallel with the Coventry Canal, so we had to turn a hairpin bend to get into it. We now had about two hours to go before we came to the eleven Atherstone locks, halfway down which we were going to load. Molly and I steered nearly all the way, but we got stemmed up several times as we were still far from being good steerers. Sometimes when these incidents happened Albert was down in the cabin, but he would come and put us right in no time. After setting us on our way again, he would quietly say 'Don't cut yer corners; there's always more water if yer keeps goin' *right* round the bend'. But Albert, we did.' 'HO no yer didn't,' and of course he was right. It sounded so easy, but somehow it was far easier *not* to take the boat close enough to the outside of the bend.

Sometimes as we went along, we would meet another pair of boats which Albert appeared to treat as if they were invisible, and we noticed that they were being worked by two men, not a couple.

Having passed them he would announce in the most withering tones, 'Them's sailors'.

'Sailors, Albert? What do you mean?'

'Sailors, didn't yer see the water can?'

'No,' rather shamefaced at not knowing why.

'Didn't yer see where it was? Behind the motor exhaust. They don't know where to put nothing, them chaps.'

This certainly gave us food for thought. How awful if in our innocence we made some similar mistake and were immediately dubbed as 'sailors'. And worse still, that the name sailor, which for me had always held a magic quality, should now have some sinister meaning. The term had originated after the first war when some unemployed merchant seamen had tried boating and had not been very popular. The tales about them were many and varied, but one of the best concerned two, who, out on their first trip alone, got as far as Blisworth tunnel but were too 'frit' to go through it, so they breasted up, put the engine ahead and sent them through on their own while they walked over the top! Naturally they got to the other side first and while they waited, along came another pair, so they told the steerer to wait as their boats were coming through. The poor man must have wondered what they were talking about, as normally there is enough room for boats to pass, but he did not have to wonder for long as he could hear the rumble of the engine, and then, sure enough, out they came, breasted up, and not a soul on board!

When we eventually got to the Atherstone locks we were disappointed to find they were narrow, as that meant extra work, so while Albert took the motor down by himself, we three were left to bring the butty on our own—two to bow-haul and one to steer. We took it in turns to do this, but it was a mixed pleasure to stand in the butty doing nothing but steer, while watching the human 'horses' tugging away on the path. We were very relieved when we found Albert waiting for us at the bottom and after being taken in tow again, we were soon tied up at Baddesley. As usual, as soon as this was done, we cleaned the outside and inside of the cabins while Albert got the holds ready for loading in the morning, and later on we made the inevitable visit to the pictures. By then, we realised that these visits were really the only outside entertainment the boaters had; otherwise it was just a session in a canalside pub, and then only if they happened to tie up early enough—and if funds permitted.

We had also become aware of how secluded and private the world was in which they lived. Being continually on the move on a highway of their own, quite separate from other forms of transport, they seldom came in contact with people other than those connected in some way with the water; their relations and friends were all boaters or ex-boaters and if any of them owned a cottage, it was naturally close to the canal. They lived with and on top of their work every minute of the twenty-four hours; they were born and died in the boats and the life they led made them resourceful, quick witted and, despite appearances, extremely sure-footed.

At Baddesley, the coal came down from the colliery in trucks and was shovelled straight out into the boats. This was the dirtiest way of being loaded, but coal dust washed off easily and once loaded, you soon had the boats smart and clean again. It was not quite so amusing bow-hauling the loaded butty up the locks again, especially as it had snowed once more, but as soon as Albert got the motor to the top, he tied her up and came back to help. He was very pleased with the order we had got this time; it was house coal for the London Co-op, which was to be unloaded just below the Cassiobury lock at Watford. We were now all right for fuel!

That night we tied up at Nuneaton, having just cleared the stop planks. We knew all about these, having met them when we were over on the Worcester cut. They are planks fitted into grooves in the stone work either side of a bridge or lock. They are slipped in one on the top of the other to form a dam so that a section of the canal or a lock can be drained for any repairs, but at this time they were being used as a precaution against loss of water should the canal be bombed. They were put in and taken out at certain hours according to the time of year.

The next day we were off early, negotiated the hairpin bend at Hawkesbury, gauged the boats and then away on the long pound to Hillmorton, which took us five and a half hours. Another three hours and we were back at Braunston. We both took turns steering through the tunnel. I remember noticing the bends very much, but that was because I was keeping well over to the right, with the result that the circle of light which was the opening would become almost obliterated—rather like an eclipse—but that taught me to keep well in the middle, and then the bends were hardly noticeable at all.

After being gauged again at Norton, we tied up at the top of the 'Bugby' locks. Albert always tried to work it so that they could tie up at Bugby because of Ciss's mum and dad, and we had a very nice evening there in the pub with all the family. It was here, too, that we first met the game 'Tip it'. Having been asked to play, I wondered very much what I had let myself in for, and to my amazement found it was the old 'Up Jenkins' of my very early school days, but minus the 'dancing crabs', 'gates with thumbs up', 'jam pots', etc. Anyway, it seemed rather odd to be solemnly playing it with all these countrymen and boaters. It was also the first time we had seen the game of skittles in a pub.

The worst of the ice was now over, for which we were very thankful, as it had prevented us from having as much practice taking the boats in and out of the locks as we would have liked. Owing to the ice, the boats needed much more skilful handling, so we had had to be content with lock-wheeling.

The next day we were at Watford and after the coal had been unloaded, we winded the boats and went back to Kings Langley for a cargo of maize for Fenny Stratford. This only took us four days and we got back to the depot on 21 March.

Chapter 7

ON OUR OWN TO LANGLEY MILL

WE HAD been with the Sibleys for five weeks, but the conditions had been unusual, to put it mildly, and though what we had learnt had been invaluable, we realised that a professional boater would never be able to allow his trip to come second to the needs of his trainees. In other words, if we stayed with Albert we would not get what we now wanted—unlimited practice in handling the boats. So the only thing to do was for us to take out a pair on our own. We put this to Mr Wood, who said that a pair would be ready for us by the end of the week and as Molly had been corresponding with two girls about coming to try the work, we fixed a time for their arrival and went to our respective homes for a little break.

On our return to Bulls Bridge we found our pair, the *Bainton* and *Saltly*, in the lay-by, all newly painted and looking very smart. But in the cabins it was different: they were as the previous boaters had left them except for having been stoved out, so sweeping up the casualties was our first task. After a motor-cabin we found the butty almost palatial. It was exactly the same as all the other butties but the depot very kindly added two small shelves for our books. This was certainly a break with tradition, but it became the one addition in the trainees' boats, and after we had all left the water I often used to wonder if any of those little shelves were still in any of the cabins as a relic of 'the girls'.

When taking over a new pair of boats, there is a tremendous amount to do in getting them ready; innumerable strings on the side cloths to be spliced—all the straps and lines to be whipped or spliced; all the equipment to be collected; the fuel oil tanks to be filled, and the batteries checked. Collecting the equipment meant going to and from the stores, fetching top cloths, shafts, water cans, cotton lines, ropes, mops, running blocks, a couple of iron stakes, a shackle or two, a T stud and of course, the windlasses. All these were to do with the outside of the boats, but the cabins were our affair; the only equipment provided being the hand-bowl and the coal box. We decided to work on the motor-cabin first, as the two trainees were to live there and it was essential for them to find a nice shining stove, new lino on the floor and everything spotlessly clean. Our own cabin would have to wait, even though the stove looked as though it were made of rust and had never been cleaned before, and after our spell with the Sibleys we knew what the standard should be.

We worked on steadily and all the most important things had been done by the time the trainees arrived. We had two more days for them to settle in and get acclimatised to the living conditions, whilst we carried on with the unending jobs, and then at last, on 1 April, we were off. The trip was a short and simple one—Harefield, only two locks above Cowley, where we were to load with ballast, then on to Leighton Buzzard, unload, and back again.

But for us it was as great an undertaking as if we had been going half way round the world. We had never even taken a pair of boats out of the lay-by by ourselves and to complicate matters there was quite a stiff breeze blowing, which is always a trial for empty boats, as being so high out of the water they can easily get blown off course. We had planned to get away by 4 o'clock and while we were briefing ourselves as to who was to do what, how and when, who should come along but Tom Sibley's wife, Lena, who confided in an undertone, 'Yer wants to use yer shaft as yer turns so as yer don't get stemmed up, there's some 'ere as wants to see yer make a mess of it'. Dear, kind, generous Lena, to bother herself about the muddle we could so easily get ourselves into, but thanks to her professional advice we edged ourselves out successfully and, thank goodness, were soon out of sight of all the watching faces.

We proceeded in a nervous manner just as far as Yiewsley, which was hardly any distance, but that was where we had tied up with Albert, so we thought it safer to spend our first night there rather than to press on into 'the unknown'. Needless to say, we made a terrible muddle over the whole procedure, but at last we got ourselves breasted up and finally tied up, and luckily no boats went by until everything was once more calm and back to normal. About our two poor trainees I remember very little; though they were referred to as trainees it was very much a case of the blind leading the blind, and it was undoubtedly a strange and bewildering experience for them. As for us, when we were at last tied up, and the engine stopped, the relief was beyond description. However, it was over, and there would never be a first time just like that again. Whatever horrors might lie ahead—and there were plenty—that one was a thing of the past.

We completed the journey to Harefield the next day, and so we should, considering it was such a short distance, but apart from steering on the straight we really were pretty hopeless. At Cowley lock, which we knew would be ready for us, we found the bottom gates closed, so we decided to breast up and I, on the butty, stupidly brought her alongside keeping to the deep water, which caused the motor to stem up. Fortunately, a man at the lock saw our predicament and came along the path with a shaft and managed to get us going again. All that of course took time, and at the next lock I brought the motor out so slowly, to make sure I would be able to pick up the butty's towing rope, that the wind caught the fore end and blew her onto the mud. Another delay.

At the next lock Molly took the motor out so fast that she missed the tow rope altogether and then had to bring the motor back. More delays, but this was the way for us all to learn and we were lucky that no other boats came along to add to our confusion.

Even when we got to the loading place things went wrong, but this was because we did not expect to see it so soon and overshot it. Anyway, we eventually tied up, and as we had to wait our turn to load we got busy doing some washing and more of the everlasting splicing. Two other pairs were there too and of course we were a great source of interest, but I do not think we committed any terrible gaffe.

The loading completed, we were faced with sheeting up on our own—a very different matter from being with Albert, and I do not know how we would have managed without the help of a small boy, the son of a crane-driver who was an ex-boatman. He was invaluable, and in fact told us exactly what to do, and by the time we finished everything looked quite presentable. We got away by 7.15 in the morning and slogged along until six, when we tied up at the Fishery lock at Hemel Hempstead. Quite a good distance considering, and as the locks were continuous, we certainly got all the practice we wanted. We were beginning to improve and by the time we had cleared the Cowroast and enjoyed the respite of Tring summit, we were getting quite confident. However, when we arrived at the Marsworth locks, we found we did not remember very much about the technique for going downhill! This put our feet back on the ground once more, and again confusion more or less took control until, luckily, the lock keeper appeared, came all the way down the towpath and told us what to do. This was a very great help and we completed the other twelve quite successfully and better still, when we got to Leighton Buzzard, where there were already five other pairs, for the first time we tied up quite well. This must have gone to our heads slightly, as after the professional tidying up of the boats, we equally professionally sauntered down the path to talk to Vie and Tommy Sibley, whom we had spotted amongst the watching faces.

I know I turned in that night feeling a little less inexperienced than ever before. However, in the morning, once again incompetence reared its ugly head, when we had to move back for the unloading and tie up on the outside. A not too difficult operation, and by putting the engine astern and shafting we got ourselves in position, but not without an incident. Instead of taking out the tiller and placing it in the hatches or on the cabin top, we foolishly put it in the steering position, with the result that when we started to move back the rudder swung round and the tiller smashed against the motor cabin top. Luckily for us, it was only the top part which broke off and we were able to steer with what remained, but it was a nuisance.

After unloading, and before we could start back for the lay-by, we had to turn round, so we went on a little further to where there was a winding hole. This was our first attempt at winding and the less said about that the better; in fact we had to have help from the one pair left waiting to unload. Luckily no other boats came along so traffic was not held up.

Once started for home we worked really hard and did not tie up until we got to Marsworth locks at 9pm. Then one more day of locks and we were back in the lay-by. Our first trip was over; it was only a short one, we had been entirely on our own, plenty of things had gone wrong, but it had given us just the right amount of harassment and food for thought, though I do not suppose we appreciated this at the time.

We were now faced with having to get another girl to join us as one of our trainees, Vivienne, had decided she would not be strong enough for the work. This left us with Rosheen, who was already 100 per cent for boating, and we just hoped that the next girl would be of the same way of thinking. We were lucky: Bridget came, and from the word go she and Rosheen got on like a house on fire, and they worked together until very nearly the end of the war. As Bridget was not able to join us at once, we had a couple of days off and went home. On our return, Albert came along in the evening and gave us all the news. He and Ciss were going to take on two more trainees—a husband and wife this time —and do a trip to Leicester with us and our two trainees buttying them.

He then proceeded to tell us exactly what we were in for. We would be loading at the Regent's Canal Dock at Limehouse, going straight to Leicester, then to Langley Mill for coal, and home again. Part of this trip would be on the River Soar. Then we would cross the Trent, with a pilot to take us over, and would experience the Erewash Canal, where, according to Albert, some of the bridges were so low that to get under them everything had to be taken off the butty cabin top, and even the tiller removed. But what fascinated us most was the twenty-mile pound; from Albert's description it was, undoubtedly, the boater's paradise. All four boats would be strung together and there would be nothing to do but wander along the towpath if you felt like it, pick flowers, gather mushrooms and blackberries or, with a ladle tied to a stick, scoop moorhens' eggs out of the nests as the boats went by. This all sounded incredible and about as far removed from our ideas of boating as it could be. Our days were never less than twelve hours of continuous activity—not physically hard all the time but nevertheless continuous movement, and with no letting up. However, by this time, we knew that Albert's stories could be so tall that they were almost out of sight, so we would just have to wait and see.

It was an interesting run down to Limehouse, passing Alperton, Park Royal, where the Guinness boats loaded, Kensal Green, Willesden, Paddington, where all loaded boats were gauged, the Maida Hill tunnel with the indentations on the roof, made by the men who had to shaft the barges through in the days before there was a tug to tow them. The more elegant surroundings of Regent's Park, with huge blocks of luxury flats on one side, some of which had been taken over by the Services, under the famous Blow Up Bridge,* through part of the Zoo, once again into a built-up area and finally the top of the locks, all of which were wide gauge and lying side by side. This helped to keep the traffic moving, as apart from all the pairs of narrow boats there were plenty of barges bringing coal and timber up from the dock. These barges were all drawn by horses in first class condition and beautifully trained. Once on the move, one horse had no difficulty in towing up to 100 tons, but to start that amount moving was a different matter. The experienced horse would begin by leaning heavily forward, then slowly swing back; he would repeat this several times and finally, when more weight was needed, he would rise up on the edge of his hooves as he leant forward with an extra effort and at last, very slowly, the barge would begin to move. These barges always worried us a lot at the beginning, they were so big, took up so much room, and moved so slowly, and to come round a bend and find one apparently stationary and completely filling a bridge hole, always used to cause slight panic. But we soon learnt to be on the watch for the nodding head of a plodding horse coming round a bend, which

---

* So called because in 1874 a boat carrying gunpowder and petroleum blew up under it.

Lines, morning and evening:
(*above*) Kit looses off the motor
so that the boats can single out;
(*below*) trainees use the same
line for the washing

Work and play: (*above*) on the way home—kicking open a gate to save a journey round the lock; (*below*) back in the lay-by, taking the bicycle off for shopping

gave warning of what to expect. In fact, my worst nightmare, at that time, was to be on a trip, going through a tunnel, getting the snubber on the blades, and being face to face with a horse-drawn barge! Once it actually did come true in every detail, but fortunately it was nothing like as bad as the nightmare, as the man with the barge knew exactly what to do and lost no time in putting things right.

It was below Paddington that we met most of the barges, and in the pound above we sometimes met a tug with a string of wide boats loaded with Paddington refuse, on their way to a rubbish dump. Compared with the barges this convoy went at quite a spanking pace, and though we were quickly past them, the stench, especially in the summer, was terrible and we felt very sorry for the men having to steer this unattractive cargo. However, there were sometimes perks to be found amongst the 'ordure'; we once saw a weather-beaten face leering out from under what had once been quite an elegant parasol!

When we eventually reached Regent's Canal Dock we found that the atmosphere there was very different from the quiet and comparative solitude of the canal up country. Noise and activity, the rattle of cranes, the coming and going of lorries, and sometimes, above it all, a burst of gun-fire. At that period all the ships had a small gun mounted in the bows and apparently they were just being tested.

The narrow boats looked very small beside all the other craft, and if there were several pairs waiting to load we would tie up alongside each other. Perhaps five or six pairs would form a solid block, and if necessary this block would be moved from one side of the dock to the other with the power from just one of the motors.

We were loaded either from the lighters or direct from the wharf and the cargo might be copper, aluminium, cement, but more often than not it was steel. On this occasion it was cement

G

in bags, but being bags of war-time quality by the time we were loaded we had a good deal covering us as well.

We were not going to let go until the morning, so after sheeting up and doing some shopping we were free for the evening's entertainments. Molly and Rosheen went to the pictures and Bridget and I paid our first visit to 'The Volunteer', the pub just outside the main gates. In those days it was illuminated by gas with a tremendously long brass gas bracket over the counter, sand on the floor and on one of the walls some interesting old prints of the canals. The atmosphere was naturally rather thick, what with the black-out and a lack of air conditioning, but especially kind and friendly, so we enjoyed ourselves and looked forward to being able to go there again.

The night was free from any air-raids. Despite all the bombing during the war the canals were comparatively free from damage. I believe there were only two instances of loss of life. We generally experienced air-raid warnings when we were in the London area, and on one occasion, in November 1944, my boats were damaged by blast. We had tied for the night just below the City lock wih Amos Grantham's pair just ahead of us. At about 8.30 there was a tremendous crack, the lights went out, and as there had been no sound of any kind beforehand I imagine it was a rocket bomb. Whatever it was caused a kind of tidal wave which broke the mooring ropes. The boats drifted apart, the factory on the corner caught fire and everything became chaos and confusion. The Granthams, lying further ahead, escaped the blast and Amos immediately came to help us. Nothing was as it had been a few moments before, except for the little fires glowing in the stoves! A new trainee on her first trip was alone in the motor cabin and had a remarkable escape, as a small object passed clean through the cabin, ripping up the handle of the kettle on its way.

In the morning we were able to see the full extent of the damage. The stables beside the path where we were tied up had caught the blast, but fortunately none of the horses were injured. All the windows in a nearby school were broken. The stands and planks had gone—some were floating in the water near enough for us to retrieve—and all the neatly rolled side cloths were hanging in ribbons.

The cabins were in the same state of chaos, so we cleared up as much as we could, and after someone from Bulls Bridge had come down to see if the hulls were still sound, we turned round and headed back to the depot for repairs.

But all that happened much later: this was our first trip down to the dock and in the morning we made an early start, Albert going first and reminding us not to forget to fill our water cans from the tap on the lock side. Fresh water supplies were few and far between and it was no joke to find the cans empty, the next tap miles ahead, and a dreary wait before we could even have a mug of cocoa. The fresh water was used for all washing purposes as well, so we were learning certain economies, like filling a hot water bottle with the vegetable water, and in the morning boiling the eggs in it, and when I boiled an egg in fresh water, I often used it to make a cup of cocoa, with apparently no ill effects.

Cocoa was always our quick hot drink, for at that time no instant coffee was to be had. In fact, we never even saw any until the first of the American soldiers came over, and they sometimes gave us some 'cute little one cup packs', which were apparently part of their normal rations.

This form of water conservancy was just one of the many side lines of boating which gradually became absorbed into the general pattern of life as we got more competent at handling the boats, which were naturally our main concern.

All the way to Leicester we were shepherded and helped by Albert and Ciss, which of course meant that we had no real responsibilities or anxieties and could concentrate on trying to memorise the route, which after Norton Junction was entirely

G*

new to us. After the Watford locks we were in the twenty-mile pound we had heard so much about, but it did not turn out to be quite such a pastoral idyll as we had been led to expect. We did all string together, but when we asked Albert why, he admitted there was really no advantage but it was 'more friendly like'. The pound came to an end at the top of Foxton locks, and I remember distinctly this first sight of them, looking down that narrow steep staircase of locks to the incredible flat expanse of the country below and wondering how on earth we were going to get both laden boats safely down to the bottom. By then Albert's pair were well under way and there seemed to be a bewildering lot of to-ing and fro-ing going on, the rattle of paddles, slamming of gates and throwing of cotton lines. By the time we were ready to start the lock keeper had taken us under his wing, and considering he had only one leg and one eye it was no mean achievement. The four of us were eager and energetic but had to be told every move, with the result that 'peg-leg' was up and down the locks, crossing over the gates, keeping an eye on both boats, rattling up the paddles, directing and explaining, showing us how to swing the cotton lines under the little foot bridges, and all with such patience and good humour that, hard work though it was, we thoroughly enjoyed the experience, which under different conditions would have been such a slog.

The rest of the journey to Leicester, Langley Mill and home again was comparatively uneventful. Everything went splendidly when we had Joe Roberts the pilot with us and when we were on our own and got into difficulties Albert was never so far away that he could not come and put things right, so I really seem to remember only the nicest things, especially the River Soar (generally called the 'Sewer'), and the lovely summer evening when we tied up at Mountsorrel, where the pub was right beside the lock. As we sat on the bench outside, listening to an exceptionally good pianist, along came a pair of empty boats which had a clothes line strung the whole length of the hold, with all the washing jigging and jogging to the rhythm and throbbing of the motor, and all in time to the music. Slowly the boats, and the washing, sank out of sight as the lock emptied, the bottom gates opened, the paddles dropped, and the beat of the motor gradually faded away in the distance.

That was one of the times which accentuated even more than usual the complete and utter contrast between letting go and tying up. As soon as the diesel engine was started up, the loud banging and beating noise was with us all day long until we tied up: even on the butty we were always aware of it. Noise, activity and keeping going were our minimum twelve-hour ration. The minute after we were tied up for the night, someone would stop the engine and at once you could almost hear the silence; we had ceased to move and our whole life changed. We got off the boats differently because they were static; we walked on the towpath differently because there was no urgency, and we lived this other life until the morning, when the engine started up again.

An old boatman once said to me 'Goo stiddy, but keep gooing', and keeping going is really the essential difference between the professional boater and a pleasure boater.

By the time we got back to Linford we were well on the way home, and that evening when we were in the pub Albert announced that he would not be seeing us again, as he was going to make a good day of it and would tie up at the Fishery* the next night, meaning that we would no longer be buttying him and could finish the trip on our own. We then and there decided that we, too, would make a good day of it and also tie up at the Fishery, even if it was midnight when we did so.

Albert was away early and at 7.15am we let go, working on

* Boxmoor, just below Hemel Hempstead.

steadily and letting our trainees get plenty of practice in taking
the boats through the twenty-three locks up to Tring summit,
which we cleared at 5pm. From then on Molly and I took over
while the others lock-wheeled, clearing the eighteen downhill in
fine style, with no hold-up of any kind, and tying up at the
Fishery at 10pm. Our reward for this achievement was Albert's
look of utter astonishment as he popped up out of the hatches to
see who we were. He was absolutely amazed, and could not
believe that there we were, and not much more than an hour
after he and Ciss had tied up.

Chapter 8

TRAINING THE GIRLS

OUR TWO trainees had now been with us for one short trip and one long one when we buttied Albert, and Molly felt that the time had come for me to take on a pair of my own, with one of our trainees as mate, while she kept the other. This we did, Bridget staying with her while Rosheen came to me, and we were then able each to take on two more trainees.

I now found myself in charge of the *Battersea* and *Uttoxeter*, feeling singularly inadequate, with a mate who knew only slightly less than I did, and two girls who knew nothing at all.

Our first trip was to Hawkesbury, where we were to get orders for coal to bring back to London, and we were to butty the others. This turned out to be a slightly embarrassing cavalcade; it was bad enough when we were only four girls in two boats, but now there were eight of us in four, and in those days the traffic, which was entirely working boats, was quite considerable. Naturally no boatman liked to be held up and delayed by amateurs; in fact, we heard that some of them took a poor view of us coming to work on the water, as they thought it might mean that they were going to be called up. Of course this was not true, as they were in a reserved occupation, but nevertheless it was essential that we got in their way as little as possible. No mean task, as our job was to teach the trainees, and they could not possibly learn without plenty of practice in handling the boats.

Off we started and before reaching Bugby both our pairs had experienced the usual string of incidents; engine trouble which in my case necessitated tying up and waiting for a fitter to come and put things right; trainees falling in, getting stemmed up, picking up various things on the blades, leaving windlasses behind at the locks, and getting water cans and chimneys knocked off while going under bridges.

In those days we were so inexperienced and eager that in moments of crisis we automatically jumped overboard, either to wade ashore with a cotton line to help pull the boat clear or grope about under the counter with a knife to cut things off the blades. Of course no boatman would have ever dreamt of doing such a thing, but then he always knew exactly what to do in any situation, and as time went on, thank goodness, we, too, found we no longer had to resort to such amateurish methods.

Sometimes we managed to stop for the night at a tie-up which was a favourite with the boaters. We then generally had a good session at the pub with them, so we were gradually getting to know a lot more of the families. By the time we had reached the top of the Bugby locks we had learnt that our orders were changed, and that instead of Hawkesbury we were to go to Leicester and Langley Mill. This was my second Leicester trip and it turned out to be my last, as during my whole time with the Grand Union I never had orders to go there again.

Doing a trip for the second time was never quite as bad as the first, but all the same there was plenty to remember during this one. The hard work it was taking the boats up the Erewash Canal, where the bridges had sunk so low, owing to the mines beneath, that we had the extra work of taking down the cratches before the boats could go under them. Most of the locks were far from being in good condition and all the way the bottom was unpleasantly near the top, so we were frequently stemmed up. Then there was the entrance to Crick tunnel, where we got the motor well and truly stuck. We wore ourselves out trying everything we knew, including our usual total immersion, and in the end had to give up. I then set out to find help, but on climbing up the embankment was faced with an expanse of country and not a soul in sight. At last two men with a tractor appeared, which they abandoned after hearing my tale and came to our assistance. Male strength was just what was needed and after some mighty heaves they got us off.

We frequently had a nagging high wind, which always seemed to blow us amongst overhanging branches which whipped and scratched along the cabin top, sweeping off anything foolishly left lying about, even knocking off the chimney and water can, and as that was something we could not afford to lose it had to be retrieved at any cost, so it was a relief when Joe Roberts joined us and released me from responsibility.

There was also the time when my brother-in-law, of quite high RAF rank, decided to join us for a couple of days and had to sleep in the open on the cargo of coal. This was because the woman at the cottage where I went to ask if they would let him sleep there replied, 'Yer don't know about people these days and we don't want none of our chickens stolen'.

By August, Rosheen, Bridget and Jill were working a pair of boats on their own. We had wondered if three girls would be strong enough to do this as though three was the usual crew for a pair, one of them was always a man—usually a husband and wife who were helped by members of their family, or sometimes they employed a lad or a girl as mate. We were very lucky that these three girls operated our first pair. Not only were they able to do the work but did it so well that they became one of the best 'pairs of galls'. Better still was the reaction of the boaters towards their success; they might so easily have been resentful, but on the contrary they were so pleased with them that they delighted in telling us, if they had happened to meet them, how well they were doing. 'That Rosie, she's a real little boater.'

This really was a good beginning, but then we had a setback: the other four, over whom we had laboured so hard, all decided to leave for various reasons. Possibly the realisation that a boater's life is not a continuous boating holiday may have had something to do with it, and they might have decided that novel and exciting as being a trainee in the summer could be, nothing was going to stop the approach of winter and the steady increase of work and responsibilities. Anyway, that put paid to getting another pair launched and operated by girls and we started off again with four new trainees.

In between trips we interviewed people who had heard about the work and wanted to come, but choosing suitable ones was not easy as those we considered promising quite often turned out to be no good, and those we thought of as being only a possible success were often a pleasant surprise. We always told them all we knew about the living and working conditions, but no amount of telling could take the place of experience, so the ones we accepted were given one full working trip, which was generally enough for them to know if they wanted to stay or not. If they did, they had one more trip, after which they had enough grounding to go off in another pair and continue their learning the hard way—by experience. Naturally enough none of us ever did stop learning, however long we stayed on the water, but that was hardly surprising as a very old man once said 'I'm a boater bred and born and I was still learning the day I retired'.

We all worked under the same conditions as the boaters and our cabins were exactly the same as theirs, except for our little bookshelves. The one difference was that the training boats were all given a spell off after each trip. This was essential as quite apart from learning the work, the trainees were also learning to live under conditions they had never experienced before, and lacking all the normal conveniences they were used to; but the girls who were working their own boats always made three consecutive trips before they had their spell of leave.

Time went on while trainees came and trainees went; sometimes, however willing and eager a girl might be she found she was just not strong enough to do the work, or perhaps because of her family she had to leave. The greatest disappointment and unnecessary waste of time was when a girl let us go on giving her the same amount of instruction as her fellow trainees for the whole of two trips, and then calmly announced she was not going to stay. However, we were fortunate in having a good nucleus of steady workers who all carried on for well over a year, and at one time we had eleven pairs working, all manned by girls.

When the war ended there were six of us still working, all of whom had joined in 1942. We used to consider that for the first year we were still only on the surface of things, but that at any time after that we began to settle down into the life and become a part of it. As far as the training was concerned, it took me well into the second year before I had developed any organised system, and up until then all the first trainees had really been training me. For those not born into the life it was different in every way from what we were used to. No two days were ever the same so there was no monotony; the life was tiring and often exhausting but if you were able to stand it, you generally became fitter than you had ever been before.

Chapter 9

THE BOATERS' LIFE

THE LIFE of a boater was a hard one. Brought up on the water, knowing no other way of life, lacking education, working for the same company, always doing the same trips, probably living on the same boat all their lives, continually doing the same work with all the added difficulties caused by the war: no wonder they used to get fed-up at times.

In contrast, we were able every now and then to go back to our homes and get a complete break, and when on the boats we were far too occupied learning and finding out about everything ever to get fed-up for the same reasons as they did.

Living in this world of their own, the boaters' friends and relations were naturally all part of the boating community, so when they wanted to visit them they seldom had to go much further than to another boat, or along the towpath to some cottage on or near the canal side.

When a pair of boats was worked by a husband and wife with a young family it was hard work for the wife, because quite apart from running the home, she was sharing and taking an active part in handling the boats. As soon as they let go in the morning until they tied up at night she was in charge of the butty, steering and doing her share of the work when going through the locks, so considerable skill and planning were needed to be able at the same time to do all the household chores as well as get all the meals prepared and cooked. If the boats were going through downhill locks, as soon as the paddles were drawn she would be back in the cabin taking advantage of the few moments whilst the lock emptied to attend to the domestic side of her life, but always ready to step up into the hatches again as soon as the bottom gates were opened and the motor started to go out. If the lock was the last one before a long pound, she might have to get her husband's dinner ready on a plate so that she could hand it over to him while the boats were still side by side. On the other hand, the meals were sometimes cooked, as well as eaten, in a long pound when the boats were separated by the long snubber, and then to get the food from butty to motor one of the children, carrying a plateful, would step onto the towpath while going under a bridge, hurry along to the next one, and as the motor went through hand it over to his dad. This method was splendid provided you were familiar with the bridges, as to get off at the wrong one might mean a weary trudge to the next, while the nice hot dinner got colder and colder.

Cleanliness also had its problems. Lack of space in the cabins and a limited water supply made things very difficult. It was much easier not to bother, and the boaters were no different from people on the shore when it was a question of being clean. Some were immaculate in themselves, their clothes and their cabins, while others were not so particular. It was always a mystery to me how the boatwomen managed to keep their blouses and 'pinners' so clean, and the children turned out in their spotless cotton frocks. In comparison, we always seemed to get in a mess so quickly. A dirty job in the engine room, a few scrabbles up a lock side and an encounter with a wet rope dragged along a muddy towpath soon put paid to what had been a clean boiler suit at the start of the day.

Shopping during a trip was also something that had to be planned; it was essential to know where the shops catering for the boat people were located, and the distances between the shops, or you might find yourself going hungry. At times, to avoid delaying the boats, a member of the crew would be sent ahead on the bicycle to get the stores and rations, so that they were all ready by the time the boats came along.

It was an exception if anything was allowed to interfere with the progress of the boats. For instance, if a pair were worked by a young couple with a baby, they would *have* to tie up while it was fed. Otherwise, the boats always came first.

When the children were quite small they spent a lot of their time sitting on the cabin tops, securely fastened to some fixture, so naturally they watched their dad steering and noticed how he worked the controls and accelerator. When they were on the butty cabin top they would notice the different shape of the tiller and the way their mum used it. So all the time they were growing up they were learning the skills of a boatman. At the first possible moment they were helping with the work; some parents took advantage of this and allowed them to do too much heavy work, but there were plenty of things they could do to help which were in no way harmful. I remember we once met a pair with apparently no one at the tiller of the motor, but as we got nearer we saw a small boy who was standing on a box which enabled him just to see where he was going and he was steering like an old professional. As we passed, his father looked out of the engine room to make sure that all was well, but there was really no need.

Another time, when I was looking down at some boats just about to leave the lock, a small child suddenly burst into tears all because her father had picked up a line instead of letting her throw it to him. These children grew up with little or no education, but they were quick witted, sure footed, extremely resourceful and so keenly observant that there was not much that they ever missed.

We often used to invite them into our cabins, and invented games that they could play. One was a form of Snakes and Ladders, with snubbers instead of snakes, and top planks for the ladders. All the hazards depicted were well known black-spots on the Birmingham route and the good things were things we appreciated, like a good road up Hatton or a favourite tie-up illustrated by a well-known pub sign. It was such a success that we were spurred on to producing an illustrated alphabet with every letter standing for something on the boats. There were plenty of things to choose from but nothing at all when we came to Q, V, X, Y, so unfortunately they had to be taken from the shore.

The slightest inaccuracies in the illustrations were pounced on at once and with great glee by the children; they missed nothing. We also noticed that if we showed them some snap-shot of the the canal, perhaps just a stretch of water with a boat away in the distance, they knew at once exactly where it was and perhaps would say something like 'why, you knows, it's just arter yer comes round that bend at the bottom of Stoke.' We certainly did not, but it was clear as daylight to them and perhaps it was just a tree or a blade of grass which had given them the clue!

As we became socially established with the boaters we visited their cabins, went to the pubs with them and were generally on good, friendly terms, but it was not until they started to play teasing tricks on us, and boating tricks which were especially designed to steal a march, that we knew we were really accepted. Sometimes, when several pairs were tied up for the night at the same place it was an advantage to be the first away in the morning so that in the event of meeting another pair you would probably be in for a good road. To achieve this advantage, if you were not the first in the line, you would wake very early and without a sound loose off the mooring ropes and, equally silently, bow-haul or shaft the boats ahead of all the others. Then, and only then, would you start up the engine which naturally woke all the others; but it was too late, by then you were well away.

GRAND UNION CANAL.

NOTICE TO STEERERS

Steerers are asked to co-operate with the Company in these difficult times, by navigating as carefully as possible and avoiding all wastage of water and damage to locks and works of the Company.

In particular, enter and leave all locks travelling **DEAD SLOW.**

Do not do any of the following :-

1. Bump or bore the gates in passing through locks.
2. Raise head or tail paddles before the gates are properly closed.
3. Waste water by running the sluices to assist you through locks.
4. Waste oil by driving into the locks too fast.
5. Start out of a full lock before opening the upper gates.
6. Bore the gates open with motor.

Remember, there are **PENALTIES** for committing navigation offences, and the Company will be compelled to enforce these penalties in the Police Courts against steerers continuing to navigate without proper care and skill.

The boatman's tricks were innumerable and all our trainees picked them up in time, so were able to hold their own, and the boaters liked them all the better for it. But we trainers had to teach all the orthodox ways, though I did point out that the right way of doing something was not necessarily the best, which always depended entirely on the prevailing conditions, and as they became more confident they soon learnt that working a lock the right way was no good when speed was all important, with all the locks in front ready and a pair behind catching up! Those were conditions when you worked every dodge you knew to keep ahead, gates were banged and rammed, water was wasted, but you did go faster.

All the boaters had a strict code of behaviour and manners, which we always respected and adopted; no one ever stepped on to or crossed another person's boat without first asking to do so, and when tied up side by side with the butty nearest the towpath, if anyone from the motor wanted to go ashore they were obliged to step across the butty hatches, and this they did while staring fixedly ahead, as even a fleeting glance down into the cabin would have been the height of rudeness. They never liked to tie up where the towpath was a popular place for people to walk, because often they were so rude as to lean over and stare right into the cabins, which was very unpleasant for the people inside. Sometimes, if we tied up with friends and were all outside having cocoa, they wouldn't hand back the mugs before first leaning down and rinsing them in the cut, and when we were with the Sibleys if Albert wanted to say something to us he was most particular always to give a good bang on the cabin side, then wait for an answer before coming over. These niceties were always observed and they were among the first things the trainees had to learn.

Chapter 10

THE WAY IT WAS THEN

IN THE summer of 1943, Molly left to start more training with Fellows, Morton & Clayton in Birmingham, and two girls went with her. As she was responsible for having started the whole training scheme, and kept things going, we now had to get someone to undertake the organising side, and were lucky to get an ex-trainee to come and do it. At about the same time three other girls, who were working their own boats, also started to train, so things were progressing, but still very slowly.

By now, trainees used to come down and stay on the boats in the lay-by for a few days to get used to the domestic side, as well as some practice in things like handling the shaft, sheeting up and taking the boats up to Cowley to see how a lock worked. Even this preliminary canter sometimes finished them off. I remember once being awakened at 2am by the girl who was sharing my cabin; she was fully dressed and packing her things ready to make her escape. Poor girl, she had all my sympathy, as she had obviously found everything too appalling to put up with; so after cups of tea and settling down for the rest of the night, she left. On looking back, it was quite amazing that none of us ever had a really serious injury, considering what a lot of dangers there were. Even the boatmen, with all their experience, sometimes had terrible accidents. A minor incident, which could happen to any of us at any time, was falling in, and funny as this generally is when it is someone else who does it, it was not so funny to cope with when on a trip. When it happened, someone would dash into the cabin to pick up the mat and remove anything that had to be kept dry, while the others helped her out. She was then shut in the cabin to remove her clothes, dry off as best she could, and dress again. Meanwhile all the clothes were wrung out and draped round the engine room to dry. Not too bad a performance if it happened in the summer and only once during the trip, but in the winter it was a different matter and we had learnt to make a thermos of cocoa while having breakfast, so that it was always ready if needed.

On one trip, it was not only needed, but had to be replenished twice more, as the three trainees fell in six times between them. One walked backwards into a full lock, one simply slipped in three times (once even when we were tied up), and the other fell once, and the other time was knocked in by the motor tiller, having just entered a lock. This could have been very nasty, but by a miracle she was not injured. It was February and dressed in a duffel coat over everything, and fleecy-lined boots, it was rather like hauling a water-logged sheep on to the counter. On that occasion her clothes had to be left with Mrs Grantham, who lived near the locks, as by then there was no available space in the engine room.

On another trip we were just about to tie up, and everything for once was under such control that one girl decided she would just have time to nip into the cabin and flour the fish we had got for our supper, so that it was all ready for cooking. Unfortunately, in her hurry, she used soap powder instead of flour. Later on, when the mistake was discovered, in her eagerness to put things right, she leant over the side to wash away the soap but leant too far, overbalanced and went in, plus plate, fish, soap and all.

But training trips were not always so full of incidents and sometimes we had enough energy left after the day's labours to go off to a dance.

Compared with the boaters we tied up for the night very early. This was something the trainers found hard to do as by then it had become a natural instinct to push on and work long hours. However, by the end of the day the trainees were tired enough, and if dragged on too far it did them no good and things were much more likely to go wrong.

I remember one day in the summer when we had tied up at the bottom of Braunston well before 6 o'clock: several pairs went by with enquiring looks at us, and then along came some friends. 'Hullo Kitty, you've tied up early—engine trouble?' It was no good trying to explain, as they had passed and were away before you hardly began. At those times the boats seemed to go very fast, but nothing like as fast as when it was obvious you were going to hit something and no amount of acceleration in reverse could possibly prevent it. Even the boaters must have thought they went too fast if they were courting: the girl in her boats might meet her young man in his and only have a few seconds to smile and exchange a word or two as they passed, followed by some lingering looks as they drew further apart, one heading for Birmingham and the other for London. But they generally managed better than that and worked their trips so that they tied up at the same place, or near enough for him to be able to bike along the towpath to see her.

The more we saw of the boaters the more we picked up their expressions, and their names for places and tie ups. We always talked about 'Noble', 'Mathus' and 'Caisey bridge' before we knew their real names were Newbold, Marsworth and Cassiobury Bridge, and we always used the boaters' form of greeting, 'How do you do?' pronounced more like 'Haa d'yer do?' and always used to people you did not know very well. Once, when we were tied up one summer evening, a man walked past on the tow path and with a nod in our direction, called out 'Haar d'yer do?' followed by 'all together'. A sure proof that he was something to do with the water, otherwise it would have been the usual 'Evening all'.

During the summer of 1944 there was a water shortage, and as a means of conservation only sixteen pairs of boats were allowed over Tring summit each day, after which certain locks were locked up with a chain and padlock fastening the bottom gate. If you failed to clear the lock, there you stayed until the next morning, by which time there would be a lot of other pairs waiting as well. We all got quite used to being 'locked up', though other people might well have been slightly shocked had they overheard a boatman say 'We was locked up with Audrey laars night at Berka'. These lock-ups were very frustrating for the boaters, though for the trainees they were often a blessing, as they meant a legitimate early 'tie up'!

Another time when there were slight delays was when the Army was having an exercise. Every bridge over the canal was guarded by a soldier and I remember chugging along very early one frosty morning and seeing these unfortunates crawling out of their sleeping bags and looking longingly at us as we went by warming our hands on the chimney, or round a nice hot mug of tea. Later on we arrived at a lock and found the top and bottom gates securely fastened and entangled with barbed wire. Loaded boats using the canal was something the army had not bargained for, so we had to disillusion them and get the obstruction removed. Another pair actually helped them to get one of their vehicles across the canal by partly lowering the boats in one of the locks, placing planks across and allowing them to drive over.

H

When we were with Albert he often used to talk about the days of the fly boats (boats which travelled non-stop, working night and day). I do not know when they ceased to operate but the nearest to them in our time were the beer boats. These pairs travelled between Park Royal and Birmingham, loading full barrels of Guinness at Park Royal, taking them to Birmingham and returning with empties. They had to work very long hours so that they kept to the strict schedule. Whichever day they loaded, they had to complete the whole trip and be ready again so that they could start off on the same day the following week. They earned good money, and certainly deserved every penny.

In contrast to being on the Beer Run, any boats passing through Grove lock were sometimes asked by the lock keeper if they would 'fetch the water'. Though he lived in a nice little house on the lock side, there was not a drop of drinking water nearer than the next lock, which was some distance away. A giant sized beer bottle, encased in a wooden frame and standing about 2ft high, was put on the cabin top and taken down to Leighton lock where it was filled with water. It was then ready to be put on the next pair that came along to take it back. Quite a satisfactory arrangement as long as the boats were not held up by ice or for some other reason.

Chapter 11

THE END OF IT ALL

I DO NOT think any of us ever thought that in a little more than twenty-five years working boats, and trade on the narrow-boat canals, would have practically disappeared. Life was far too real and exacting for more than the occasional fantasy about the future. I do remember one evening, though, when we were all crammed into our hot, stuffy little cabin and let ourselves go on planning what we considered the ideal comforts for a trip when the war was over. A bathroom with hot and cold taps, fitted carpets, a Hoover, a telephone, and every impossible suggestion followed by roars of laughter. This mythical trip was, apparently, to be without a cargo, as we were just going to tie up when and wherever we liked, and we would *never* work through any locks unless we felt like it. Incredibly funny as it sounded then, all those things have actually happened, but as far as I am concerned there is only one kind of canal boating; possibly it's a case of 'once having tasted blood'.

Not very long after leaving the water I did spend a short holiday in a motor cruiser on the Llangollen canal. My poor

companion had to put up with a lot as old habits were far from
dead, and I forced her to carry on despite torrents of rain, drag
on to the top of locks when there was not the slightest reason
why we should not tie up in the middle, and to work on far too
late in the evenings. One night I was roused by another passing
pleasure boat and automatically, almost in my sleep, actually
called out 'How many locks have you made ready?' I was vaguely
conscious of a startled and rather horrified face gliding past the
window before sinking back to sleep. Canal boating had certainly
taken a hold of me. It was a way of life which, provided you
stayed long enough to get over the first novelty and excitement,
got into your very being. Despite the hardships and many disadvantages, there was a great deal to be said for the lessons it
taught, and this is borne out by many an ex-boater today, who,
since leaving the water, is now leading a totally different kind
of life.

One of the features of a well kept, smart pair of boats was the
dazzling whiteness of any ornamentation made by cotton lines.
The black tarpaulin over the cratch was held in place by lines
complete with neat coils and canvas bands, all whiter than white,
and the strange thing was that this whiteness was produced by
nothing but constant scrubbing with cut water. I remember
being told this by Rose Jackson and I found it hard to believe,
but it was true. Whitening as used for tennis shoes, or pipe clay,
were things quite unknown to the boater, apart from the inevitable shortages of many things. These shortages often put tremendous value on the most surprising things; one of my proudest
possessions was about an inch of steel wool, which was only
produced when any brass work was beyond the powers of Blue-
bell. It was a strange thing that we were issued with brass cleaning material so that we could keep our brass bands and chains
gleaming and glittering, when everything else throughout the
country was blacked out and darkened. Not a chink of light must

be shown from a cabin slide, or a slightly open cabin door, but the moon could wink and sparkle all over our shining brasses!

A lot of the chains on the chimneys were not just ordinary chains but much more elaborate, and being anxious to have the same, I asked a boatman where they came from. The answer was simple. When you were taking your coal to Croxley Mills you only had to go to one of the sheds open to the canal, where there was a mountain of army canvas gas-mask cases. All the cases had brass buckles and clips, and you simply cut off the clips which could then be linked together and there was your chain. It was only a matter of time before we were unloading again at Croxley and I had the opportunity of climbing up this unusual mountain. Sure enough there were clips and buckles galore, and I took my time tramping about amongst them and selecting the ones I liked best and cutting them off. While doing so, a pair of boats went by, so I waved merrily, indicating what I was doing by holding up my lengthening chain. Funnily enough it was the very man who had told me what to do, but to my surprise he quickly turned away and gazed into the distance. How dim could I be? It was only then I realised that this was loot of the highest degree. It had all seemed so open and natural, and that when all those thousands of cases were going to be turned into paper, it was such a pity that just a few of the clips should not be put to a useful purpose. However, it was impossible to put the clips back and I still have those handsome chains to this day.

There were other occasions, too, when we apparently received the cold shoulder from boaters. This was when not far from a flight of locks we met another pair, and as we passed we would call out 'How many have you made ready?' Sometimes the answer was 'N'air a one', and then we knew that there was another pair not far ahead of us. At other times there was no answer at all, just a concentrated stare at perhaps the water can, or into the distance, and we were very disconcerted by this the first time it happened, thinking we must have said quite the wrong thing to the wrong people. However we learnt later on that a glance back, soon after passing, would show that all was normal again and the boatman would be looking back at us while holding up his hand with fingers extended to indicate the number. Instead of ignoring us he had been trying to remember exactly where he had met the last pair, after which the remaining locks would be in our favour. When the same question was put to me, I found it extremely hard to give an accurate reply, and often the thought process took so long that the questioner's boats were out of sight before I had worked out the answer.

When starting to work on the Grand Union, and meeting far more working boats and their crews, I used to think how strange it was that so many of the men seemed to be slightly hump-backed. However, the hump was quickly removed when they whipped out their windlass, which had been worn over their shoulder and inside the back of the jacket! When jackets were not worn, it was generally kept in the belt at the back with the angle downwards. Women, more often than not, wore it in the front—possibly owing to the difference in male and female waist lines.

The men always steered the motor and were known as Steerers, never Captains. For instance, when in the lay-by at Bulls Bridge waiting for orders, you would hear over the loudspeaker, 'Steerer so and so, boat number so and so, you are wanted in the office for orders'. It was always quite a moment when we heard *our* name, and our boat number, for the first time.

On the Grand Union the one exception to the man steering the motor was Mrs Sammy Saxon. I had wondered why she was continually on the motor while Sammy, who was rather small, looked like a troll hunched up in the hatches of the butty, but the boats were in her name and not in Sammy's.

The Saxons, like many other couples whose families had

grown up, often had a dog as a pet, which they treated just like a child. We once saw them come into a lock and as Mrs Saxon stepped off the motor to shut the gate, Nigger jumped off behind her. But it had just started to pour with rain so she turned to him and said 'Run along out of the rain, babby, run along in, my duck', and Nigger at once jumped back on to the counter and down into the cabin.

Then there were the Brays, whose dog was called Toby, and whom we once met when we had a small puppy with us which was sitting on the cabin top. As we passed we pointed to the puppy and the size of it seemed to amuse Mrs Bray very much and she leant down to speak to someone in the cabin. To our surprise up jumped Toby, and Mrs Bray, with her arm around him, pointed to the pup and said 'Look at the little babby, Toby, look at the babby'.

A real boat dog was as much at home on the boats as the most experienced boatman. He knew the right moment to jump off and when to jump on, he kept out of the way of the straps and lines, and he knew when a rope was taut and safe to scratch his back against. I often saw a dog jump off the counter of a motor going into the lock, sniff round the first checking stump, run round the balance beam, and step back on to the cabin top just as it was level with the lock side. The Smith's family dog was called Bob and one day he and Jim went off to lock-wheel up Hatton, but at the third lock, when it was still emptying, Bob somehow managed to fall in. Jim wondered how he could make him understand that he would just have to wait until the bottom gates opened, then swim out and get on to the path, but Bob looked around and thought of a better plan. Up he swam to the top of the lock, climbed out on to the cill and sat there waiting for the boats! As soon as the motor came in he jumped on to the deck, up on to the top planks and trotted back to the cabin.

Besides dogs there were several cats, some canaries, rabbits,

and a ferret or two. The rabbits had quite a good time as when
the boats were empty they were often allowed to have the run of
the cargo space. Some boats even had chickens; the first one I
saw had been let out of its hutch and was on the cabin top
pecking away at some food in a saucer, which looked very odd,
but not half as odd as the four fat old hens who were scratching
and picking about on the cargo of coal in the boats beside which
we tied up one evening. The ferrets were undoubtedly to help
with the sporting side of life. 'I'm fair sick o' pheasant' was the
casual remark made by a boatwoman one day when we were all
chatting together. Pheasant! We had almost forgotten there were
such things, but later on we learnt that a certain boatman always
left his family to take the boats up one of the flights of locks,
while he and his dog (possibly the ferret too) disappeared into
the countryside. By the time he rejoined the boats at the top
lock he generally had something for the pot!

The popular idea about canal boaters was that they led a slow
and leisurely life, and this was quite understandable because
people seldom had more than a glimpse of the boats when they
were going along a pound. Even if they watched them working
through a lock it would be impossible to realise what it was like
to go through the same routine perhaps thirty or forty times a
day. The average speed of a pair of boats was about four miles an
hour, taking into consideration the amount of cargo carried, the
depth of the pounds and the number of locks through which
they had to work. There was seldom enough water to enable the
boats to go any faster, and in any event the banks would not have
been able to stand up to the wash. A pair of boats carrying the
equivalent of four or five trucks of coal would average 4 to $4\frac{1}{2}$
days from Coventry to London depending on where they loaded
and where they were to unload.

In the early days of the canals, where there were passenger
boats as well as cargo, and all were horse-drawn, speed was of

great importance, especially as the passenger boats were in direct competition with the stage coaches.

As early as the 1830s, experiments were carried out with specially designed light boats, which proved that when the speed was increased beyond 4mph, which built up a low wave, the boats rose in the water, passed the wave and travelled smoothly at about 10mph. Eventually the horse-drawn boats gave way to steam and steam in turn gave way to the diesel engine. But the boatman remained the same and always knew plenty of dodges besides the actual speed of the boats to enable him to make a fast trip. In fact he could usually find some way round to avoid what he considered was a quite unnecessary rule or regulation.

As time went on and we settled more deeply into the life there was much more opportunity to observe and speculate. For instance, about the origin of the boat people. Were they originally gipsies, and how did their distinctive paintings and designs originate? Were the first boatmen men who had helped with the actual making of the canals and were their castles painted on the boats the result of some wag who, for a joke, painted the first one?

Brindley was laughed to scorn and jeered at for planning to build his first aqueduct over the River Irwell, and an eminent engineer is quoted as saying 'I have often heard of castles in the air but never before saw where one of them was to be erected'. If true it is quite possible that it was talked about by all the workers, and who knows, perhaps the first boat to cross the Barton aqueduct did so proudly sporting a castle, so 'the floating castle in the air' had become a reality.

All the boaters we met, without exception, considered it the greatest slur to be thought of, or even compared to, gipsies. Many a time I have tried to explain that it was just because of all the bright colours and shining brasses that people were reminded of gipsies, and also because they were continually on the move. Admittedly they did sometimes look rather gipsy-like, but no wonder when the greatest part of their lives was spent in the open air. Anyway, gipsy was not a word ever to be mentioned.

In our part of the country there were other words, too, which were never used; these were the familiar nautical terms like port and starboard. To the boatman everything was either left or right, or inside or outside, the inside being the part of the canal nearest the towpath and outside away from the path. As the towpath frequently changes sides, the inside could be either left or right, so instead of being told to port or starboard your helm the order would be 'hold out' or 'hold in'. Oddly enough the wooden uprights, which were used to support the top planks were often marked with a P & S, but if the boatman knew what the letters were he was not likely to know what they stood for. We did not 'moor' or 'loose off' either, but simply 'tied up' and 'let go'.

The fact that so many of the boatmen were not able to read was by no means such a disadvantage and handicap as one might imagine. He would never let on about it, and being so keenly observant and having such a retentive memory he got by in a quite remarkable way. For instance, one of the boatmen used to get himself from Bulls Bridge to Paddington by train, and then on to Paddington basin where he had to pick up some boats, and another, who had left the water and was living in London after the war, often cycled a considerable distance right across London to come and have tea with me. I cannot think how many signs and indications I would have had to rely on to make the same journey.

Being such great picturegoers, I sometimes used to think they must often find themselves seeing the same films over again, but they were far too spry for that and always carefully studied the stills outside before buying their tickets.

Most of the boaters we knew are now off the water, and the children we knew are now married with children of their own growing up in conditions very different from those of their parents, which despite the many disadvantages—or perhaps because of them—produced such a resourceful independence of spirit. Today the canals can be compared with the new edition of a very old book which has been out of print for many years; there are a lot of new illustrations, and the layout has changed considerably, but this book is now wide open for everyone to enjoy. The days of the old edition have gone forever, but they will always live on in the memories of all those who had a share in them.

INTRODUCTION

IT WAS in the autumn of 1945 that Eily (always known as Kit) Gayford first wrote to me. I had produced a book called *English Rivers & Canals* in the old 'Britain in Pictures' series, and because of it she suggested we should meet. I was just married, and scarcely settled in a war-damaged little house in Paddington. Kit ate dinner off a packing case with a cloth on it and talked as only Kit can, putting all of herself into every sentence. I don't think she realised how small she was making me feel, for after her five years of life on the boats she knew so much more about canals than I did.

Thenceforward we were firm friends. Three occasions stand out: a winter evening spent visiting boaters, whose craft was moored in Regent's Canal dock, ending at the 'Volunteer', in the days when it was gas-lit and sawdust-floored; an excursion to Brentford depot, and the fish and chip supper we had there; and Kit lockwheeling for my wife and myself on the Grand Union all the way from Nash Mills up the locks past Berkhamsted to Marsworth.

Now Kit lives on a houseboat moored off Cheyne Walk, and from her stern window she can see the river fire station at Battersea where I spent part of the war. She must be on the water, for the story she has told in this book made her into a boatwoman. I have had great pleasure from reading this book in manuscript, and now it is in print it will take to each reader, along with the story, a little of Eily Gayford's personality.

CHARLES HADFIELD

APPENDIX

THE BOATMAN'S NAMES FOR THE LOCKS BETWEEN THE DOCK AT LIMEHOUSE AND BIRMINGHAM

Commercial lock
Sammons Lane
Johnsons
Mile End
Longford
Actons
Sturts
City Road
St Pancras
Hampstead Rd. 3
Cowley
Uxbridge
Denham
Widewater
Black Jack
Copper Mill
Springwell

Stockers
Rickey
Walkers
Croxley
Caisey Bridge
Iron Bridge
Albert's 2
Lady Capels
Hunton Bridge 2
Hunton Chain
Five Paddle
Kings Langley
Nash 2
Apsley 3
Boxmore
Fishery
Slauters

Bottom Winkwell

Middle Winkwell

Top   „

Sewerage

Bottom Side

Top Side

Sweeps 2

Broadwater

Gas 2

Bushes

Northchurch

Dodswell 2

Cowroast

Mathus 7

Peters 2

Nags Head 3

Corketts 2

Pools

Neals

Church

Grove

Leighton

Stoke Hammond 3

Talbots

Finney

Cosgrove

Stoke Bruan 7

Bugby 7

Braunston 6

Wigrams 3

Itchington 10

Radford 10

Warwick 2

Hatton 21

Knowle 5

On page 63 I say that Albert took the motor in on the right of the butty, whereas Mr A. J. Lewery in his title-page drawing shows it on the left. I worked on motors with National engines. These were fitted with reduction gear; their propellers therefore threw them towards the right-hand wall, so leaving the rest of the lock clear for the butty. Mr Lewery has illustrated a motor with a Bolinder direct drive engine. This enters a lock on the left, as its propeller throws it towards the left-hand wall.

Heather Bell loading flour at Worcester (*above*),
and waiting to load coal at Cannock (*below*)

<u>MINISTRY OF WAR TRANSPORT</u>

Dear Madam, ...194.

<u>Training Scheme for Women</u>

Thank you for your letter.   The Training Scheme for women is briefly as follows:-

Training takes from 2 to 3 months, according to individual ability, and during that period you will learn the entire management of a pair of boats - the motor boat and the butty (the butty being the one which is towed by the motor).   You will live, eat and sleep on the boats, which will be travelling along the canal routes carrying actual cargoes.   In addition to being taught how to operate the boats you will be shown the correct methods of loading and unloading, care of cargo, sheeting up, etc. and will be given a certain amount of instruction in the care of the engine.   It is emphasised, however, that boatwomen are not expected to be mechanics and all repairs are carried out by experienced fitters employed by the Canal Company; also, normally speaking, you will not be required to load and unload your cargoes, but only to assist.

During training you will be paid at the rate of £2 per week, and out of this you will have to pay for food, state insurance and any personal outgoings.   When reporting for training ration books should be brought with you, when arrangements will be made with our local Food Committee to issue Emergency Coupons which enable purchases to be made in any part of the country, and there is no difficulty in obtaining supplies.   Whilst training, one week's leave will be granted without pay at the conclusion of each trip, which should take about three weeks.   When considered proficient and able to operate boats without supervision, trainees will be appointed to boats of their own, a crew consisting of three women, there being no objection to friends going together.

It must be realised that although the work is not particularly arduous, long hours are worked over a seven-day week, and this together with exposure to the weather makes it imperative that only women of robust constitution and good health should enter this employment.

Ministry of War Transport standard letter
to applicants for Training scheme (front)

When you have completed your training and become one of a crew you will work under the same conditions as all the canal boatmen, payments being at freight rates agreed between the Canal Carriers and the Transport & General Workers' Union of so much per ton, according to the class of cargo and distance travelled, etc. // The earnings of a pair of boats should amount to about £10 or £11 per week, and it must be distinctly understood that this has to be shared between the three persons forming the crew. // The Carriers guarantee minimum earnings of £3 per week for each member of the crew when operating boats on completion of training. It should be emphasised, however, that your earnings are dependent largely on your own efforts.

When operating your own boats, the following arrangements will apply regarding leave.

No leave will be granted after the first trip, but on completing the second trip three clear days will be given. After a further two trips six clear days, and they and 6 respectively, without pay on the completion of each second and fourth trip. This concession, however, is entirely dependent upon whether the services of the boats and crews can be spared for these periods and leave is granted subject to your keeping in touch with this office during leave and that you may be liable to recall if necessary. One week's leave with pay will be allowed each year.

Transport is an essential key to Victory, and by entering this industry you will be carrying out essential work of great importance.

Yours faithfully,

M. ERMS (MISS)

Supervisor,
MINISTRY OF WAR TRANSPORT,
TRAINING SCHEME FOR WOMEN.

Ministry of War Transport standard letter (back)

The author teaching a trainee, Miranda Pemberton-Pigott,
how to splice

Audrey

THINGS TO REMEMBER

"Boats come first"

Keep going but go steady.

A good crew gives a perfect example of cooperation & team work.

Try to use at least one more chad

Try to be in the right place at the right moment.

Never walk on the boats or one to go into that lorry or shed from within which to catch hold of something in case you slip.

When you use anything always put it back in its right place.

When you use boats make a point of finding out where all equipment is kept.

If you notice that something is always used in a fixed order or a certain way then train to do it at once. Make a list of that later what can be done that way first.

Never leave a rope on the kitty catch when crossing the towing path.

When the boats are tied up always tie up at the motor, tiller & round the kitty tiller.

In boats, use the mooring tie up with a rocket stake, which will round the mooring to avoid it's mooring class.

Be careful that it's alert.

FISHERY - COW ROAS

SLAUGHTERS. LW

BOTTOM WINKWELL. L.W Swing bridge

MIDDLE WINKWELL, L.W.

TOP WINKWELL. L.W.

SEWERAGE. L.W.

BOTTOM SIDE. L.W.

TOP SIDE. L.W

SWEEPS 2. L.W   Ship at 2' (latch first rate)   T.U. below 1st middle on clear 2' about 9' Clept 9 places W. at 2'

BROAD WATER. L.W.

GAS 2. L.W

BUSHES. L.W.

NORTH CHURCH L.W.   T.U. above middle W.

DODSWELL 2. L.W Ship at 1.1' Turned middle of ferry   middle from from hill steep

COW ROAST. Trip canal W. Change to clean

TRING SUMMIT. at least 1 hour use towing rope

COW ROAST. If you have difficulty in getting your boat into the lock, it is the motor back till the bows are level with the boat astern to bring her a boat [?] in.

Down hill. Be sure to let the boat load before the lock is quite empty, as you cannot fill if you are on the bottom & unable to do so. It may be necessary to slow up if the speed [?] out.

Stop the motor out.

PRIMUS

Keep Primus clean & filled.
If a silent burner, clean out the bur
regularly, & see it will work before fun.

How to Light Primus

Get the Primus away from any draught
or wind. Fill cup & let it fill with meths.
Light meths & close valve.
When meths is nearly burnt away
give about 6 pumps. It should then
burn finely with a blue flame &
morning noise, the metal circle getting
red hot & even.
If the flame is yellow like a candle,
or un-sild, light a spill from the
flame & un-prick her. Re-light anew
& it you do not get a blue flame
repeat pricking process.

Lentil Pie

Soak a cupful of lentils & ¼ cup of
rice for about 12 hours.
Add pepper & salt & boil gently till
soft. Dry mins, great & cook
& make 2 brown.
Add some great cheese & crumbs &
butter & mix in the omenet.
Put in dish or casserole with
mashed potatoes. Cover lightly & all
in oven or stove.

Fish Pie

Smoke ¾ lb cheap fish. 1 lb salmon.
Grease a dish. the liquid. Mix in small
potatoes & mash together. Form & dredge
with a little milk.
Put in dish or casserole, but cream
fried bacon & turn every thing when
of bread, brown & finish.

Trainees at Bulls Bridge: from left to right (*above*):
the author, Audrey, Mary, Frankie Campbell-Martin,
Evelyn Hunt, and Anne

Frankie Campbell-Mar[...]
and Evelyn Hunt (abov[...]
pipe-smoking
trainee (below)

WEDNESDAY
~~MONDAY~~—April 1st, 194~~0~~2 .
Registered Design No. 668,615

Sun rises 5.37 ; sets 6.32   Lighting up 7.2   High Water London Bridge 8.31 a.m. ; 8.51 p.m.

A lovely brilliant morning & having found we had really got all our gear M went to Mr Wood to ask if we couldn't get away just for a short trip, & as he said yes we decided to let go after lunch. Les came along as we were starting up the engine & then one of the valves stuck; very lucky really as they sent a fitter round to put it right — this all took time & in the middle it was the mens tea hour, but as Mrs Moll turned up to see us just then, it fitted in all right. At about 4.45 M & I let go with the motor to take her round to be bunkered. Before this dear Lena had come up to me & said "You wants to shaft er round as you turns so as she doesn't get stemed up; theres a lot as what wants to see you make a mess of it." I thought it terribly nice of her & as there was a very high wind went up to the fore end with the shaft. After making fast at the oiling place I went back to the butty. We eventually let go at 5.20 Les Curtis & everyone to see us off. The wind was awful & after steering an erratic course we decided to tie up at Greenslade which we did at   . We made an awful mess of it but thank goodness there was noone there to see us & the relief when we were actually tied up was terrific! Had been feeling as nervous as I used to be for a stage appearance! Our trainees were all right, ~~though~~ I think it must be confusing for them beeing trained by such inexperienced people as we are.
It was good of old Moll to come down & see us & everyone else to give us such a good send off.

Page from author's diary for 1 April 1942

THURSDAY
~~TUESDAY~~—April 23rd, 1942

Sun rises 5.48; sets 8.10   Lighting up 9.10   High Water London Bridge 3.16 a.m.; 3.40 p.m.

Let go at 7 AM & we continued with our meander, first coming to a tunnel & then Foxton locks (10). They were really delightful. A one legged & one eyed lock keeper with such a well kept house & garden. A pig in a spotless stye & a rabbit, clipped grass all round the lock. The locks are fascinating. It is a 75 ft drop & 30 years ago there used to be a lift for the boats, but now there are 5 direct lift locks, a short pond in which you can pass, & then 5 more, single they are for single boats. After that the rest of the pound then 5 more locks, a short pound & we tied up at Newton at 7.25.

We were really much better today, but the whole trouble is that we are all right as long as things are right but when they are not we just don't know what to do.

22
23
24
25
26
27
28
29

Page from author's diary for 23 April 1942

Summer idyll

Working pairs (*above*);
being filmed in September 1945 (*below*)

Denham Deep Lock (*above*);
working on the tow rope (*below*)

Working pairs: taking a bend above Uxbridge Lock (*above*); at Cowley Lock (*below*)

News & Chronicle

No. 30,775   WEDNESDAY, JANUARY 3, 1945   ONE PENNY

Woman who trains bargees is in Honours list

AND MAN WHO PUSHED GOERING BACK

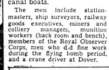

THE second part of the New Year Honours List, published today, gives names of 1,070 civilians signalled out for reward for their work which helped to make D-Day possible.

There are 200 O.B.E.s (18 women), 371 M.B.E.s (77 women) and 489 British Empire Medallists (59 women). There are also ten commendations for valuable service in the air.

A wide variety of people and occupations is covered. Women range from the driver of Gen. Eisenhower's car to foster-mothers of evacuated children and the principal trainer of women crews for canal boats.

The men include station-masters, ship surveyors, railway goods executives, miners and colliery managers, munition workers (back room and bench), members of the Royal Observer Corps, men who did fine work during the flying bomb period, and a crane driver at Dover.

Miss Eily Gayford, M.B.E.
Trains women for canal boats

From the *News Chronicle* 3 Jan 1945

TUESDAY 4ᵗ DEC:

Dave brought me a mug of tea at 6:30.
Packing & packing. Everything white with frost.
At last got everything cleared from the butty.
Am glad these men are taking the boats, they are
so nice & clean & I should have hated to leave
the Buttermere & Dane just empty in the Long Bay.
Was able to say good bye to the Brookes, James,
Tommy Sibley & the Wises & was so pleased when
Mrs Brookes said "Oh we shall miss the gals."
Took a lot of things up to Bert for disposal. All the
money he gets for the clothing is to go to the R A F
Association. Good byes to everyone & after my
last dinner in the canteen & final settling in the
Office left in the van with Mr Peters for Liverpool
Street. On arrival there they would not take the
crate so on we had to go to Bishopsgate. After
Mr Peters had gone I went back to L P S. & put the
other things in the cloak room. So that's the end
of my career as a canal boat woman.

Page from author's diary for 4 Dec 1945

GRAND UNION CANAL CARRYING CO., LTD.

DIRECTORS:
E. J. WOOLLEY
JOHN MILLER
W. K. SIMPSON
C.Saywood

HEAD OFFICE
PORT OF LONDON BUILDING
SEETHING   LANE.   E.C.3.
TELEPHONE ROYAL 5630
(10 LINES)

Temporary Address:

TRANSPORT   HOUSE,

Our Ref...JM/AC....   RESERVOIR   ROAD,   RUISLIP,   MIDDX.   ....Your Ref.

TELEPHONE AND TELEGRAMS RUISLIP 4081

23rd May, 1945.

Miss E. Gayford,
c/o Bulls Bridge Depot.

Dear Miss Gayford,

Now that the War in Europe has come to an
end I hasten to convey to you my wholehearted thanks for
the excellent work and devoted service which you have
given in the company's interest over the past five years
which have been so full of difficulties of one kind and
another.

Your unfailing courage must have been a
source of great inspiration to those working with you,
and your very gallant efforts are very much appreciated
by us all.

Our company has made a fine contribution
to the War Effort, and this could not have been done if
it had not been for the fine, wholehearted work of our
staffs, and on behalf of the Board I would like to give to
you my wholehearted thanks.

Yours sincerely,

CHAIRMAN

A letter from the Chairman of the GUCCC

INDEX

Boat names are shown in SMALL CAPITALS,
pages numbers of illustrations in **bold**.